# BUILDING EFFECTIVE SOCIAL WORK TEAMS

How has social work changed over the years? What are some of the best social work teams doing differently to meet the complex practical and emotional needs of service users? What practical tools and approaches can social work managers implement with their teams? Dr. Judy Foster examines good social work practice and the supporting factors that are essential to underpin social work teams – coherent policies; well-qualified and motivated staff; good management support structures; delegated autonomy and discretion for social workers; and mental space to allow reflective and creative problem solving.

She illustrates the dilemmas and rewards of social work relationships through personal stories from her own career as a social worker, manager and teacher – and interviews with social workers and managers. These examples show the relationship between 'doing' something for someone and 'being' emotionally present to empower a service user to manage better. The book is intended to help social work managers improve the support environment for their teams – and hence their effectiveness – and to inform students and others in related professions interested in learning more about social work. It will also have a wide appeal to an international social work readership.

**Judy Foster** is an experienced social worker and manager. She is a visiting lecturer in social work at the Tavistock Clinic, teaching postgraduate students. She trained as a child care officer before becoming a generic social worker, and managing the first referral and assessment team for a large inner city social services department. Subsequently she was head of training and staff development for the department, providing development opportunities for senior managers, social workers and care staff – introducing innovative projects in management, adult care, mental health, and children and families.

She was a national project officer at the Central Council of Education and Training in Social Work developing training standards in mentoring skills and care for children and young people; and at Skills for Care developing national training standards in mental health. She founded the Social Perspectives Network in modern mental health – and was chair of St Michael's Fellowship, which provides residential parenting assessments to family courts and supportive work with young parents in the inner city. Her doctorate in social work was awarded in 2009. She is married with two children and three grandchildren.

# BUILDING EFFECTIVE SOCIAL WORK TEAMS

*Judy Foster*

Routledge
Taylor & Francis Group

LONDON AND NEW YORK

First published 2017
by Routledge
2 Park Square, Milton Park, Abingdon, Oxon OX14 4RN

and by Routledge
711 Third Avenue, New York, NY 10017

*Routledge is an imprint of the Taylor & Francis Group, an informa business*

© 2017 Judy Foster

*British Library Cataloguing in Publication Data*
A catalogue record for this book is available from the British Library

*Library of Congress Cataloging in Publication Data*
Names: Foster, Judy (Social worker), author.
Title: Building effective social work teams / Judy Foster.
Description: Abingdon, Oxon ; New York, NY : Routledge, 2017. | Includes bibliographical references and index.
Identifiers: LCCN 2016026358| ISBN 9781138230088 (hardback) | ISBN 9781472480828 (pbk.) | ISBN 9781315387062 (ebook)
Subjects: LCSH: Social service—Practice—Great Britain. | Social workers—Great Britain. | Social work administration—Great Britain.
Classification: LCC HV40.8.G7 F67 2017 | DDC 361.3068/4—dc23
LC record available at https://lccn.loc.gov/2016026358

ISBN: 978-1-138-23008-8 (hbk)
ISBN: 978-1-4724-8082-8 (pbk)
ISBN: 978-1-315-38706-2 (ebk)

Typeset in Bembo Std
by Swales & Willis Ltd, Exeter, Devon, UK

MIX
Paper from
responsible sources
FSC
www.fsc.org    FSC® C013985

Printed in the United Kingdom
by Henry Ling Limited

# CONTENTS

# ILLUSTRATIONS

## Figures

## Tables

# FOREWORD

Social workers are the first to be blamed when child tragedies occur, but society still expects them to provide expert help and support for families and adults in trouble. How then can we attract able people into social work to shoulder this responsibility, when society appears to undervalue the profession – and how can we motivate and retain them?

With her extensive experience as a social worker, manager and teacher, Judy Foster is in a strong position to offer insight into the way forward. She tells the story of the changes in social work practice over the last forty years based around her own experience with service users, against a background of major changes in our increasingly multi-racial society. Judy highlights the changes in peoples' attitudes towards public services – and desire for greater coherence between health and social care provision to take account of the well-being of the whole person. She vividly illustrates how core social work values have been maintained across a generation, but recognises the considerable pressures that current social workers have to contend with due to austere financial constraint, modern complex legislation, and an adversarial professional and political climate.

On reading Judy's book I was struck by three particular features: firstly, the wealth of personal accounts of professional experience embedded within a book that is simultaneously full of rich theoretical insight and practical advice for managers; secondly, the power of personal stories that illustrate wider social experiences; and thirdly, the complex relationship between individuals' lives and their immediate context, whether that be families in their social and domestic setting or professionals within their work organisation. In essence these features encapsulate for me what we mean by the 'psychosocial' – a coming together of external and internal worlds, of cognitive and affective understanding and experience and the integration of the psychological and the sociological.

Judy's long career as a social worker, a career that is characterised by a deep respect for people and an equally deep commitment to psychodynamically informed practice, epitomises for me a psychosocial approach and this is its strength and the strength of this book – a publication that is both profoundly personal and profoundly theoretical as well as practical. And it is this inextricably interlinked relationship between the head-theory and the heart-experience that distinguishes this book from others in the field.

I warmly commend it to social work practitioners, managers and students, and to other professionals working in allied fields, as it offers a compassionate, reasoned and realistic understanding of the challenges faced on a daily basis by individuals experiencing distress and vulnerability, and those seeking to support and empower them.

Gillian Ruch
Professor of Social Work, University of Sussex

# PREFACE

This is a story of the changes in social work during my career. It examines good social work practice, and the supporting factors that underpin social work teams. It is intended to help social work managers improve the support environment for their teams – and to inform students and others interested in learning more about social work. It is based on my personal experience as a social worker, manager and teacher – and on a multiple-case study of three social work teams working with vulnerable adults.

Over the years there has been public and political pressure to put greater emphasis on throughput of cases with targets for service delivery, rather than interventions supporting the complex practical and emotional issues of service users. This trend needs to change with social work teams properly supported and empowered to find long-term solutions for the growing number of service users.

I studied three inner city teams – one helped younger adults with illness or disability in the community, another arranged care for people discharged from hospital, and the third supported homeless mentally ill people. The findings confirmed my experience as a manager that five factors are essential to help social work teams function well – coherent national and local policies; well-qualified and motivated staff; good management support structures; delegated autonomy and discretion for social workers; and mental space allowing reflective and creative problem solving. This book explains why the organisation of social work needs to take more account of these factors.

Chapter 1 covers my personal experience as a social worker and manager, and currently as a teacher of postgraduate social work students. It touches on some of the major changes in national policies that I have seen during this time.

Chapter 2 sets out the emotional issues of service users, and types of intervention that social work can provide. Chapter 3 focuses on how social workers relate to service users, reflect on their lives and decide interventions. Chapter 4 records actual day-to-day practice in the three different social work teams, and the unconscious elements of the work from my view on the boundary of the teams. Chapter 5 indicates the methodology that I used to analyse the quality of the support environment for the social work teams.

The evidence for each factor is assessed in Chapters 6–10, along with ideas suggested for managers to develop their teams. Chapter 11 compares social work practice today with that of the 1970s. Chapter 12 considers the implications for all those concerned with the management and delivery of social work. It challenges social work managers to appraise the quality of support that underpins their teams and consider if changes can be made to generate improvements in performance.

Judy Foster

# ACKNOWLEDGEMENTS

I would like to thank all my professional colleagues over the last four decades for their support and encouragement – especially Clare Parkinson and Andrew Cooper at the Tavistock Clinic. I am also grateful to the three social work teams for letting me observe and reflect on their work with vulnerable adults. Their good humour and professionalism illuminated the research, while their candid responses allowed me to explore the hidden and disturbing aspects of the work that they contain and manage for society.

There are many others who have helped – friends, my family; and most importantly the service users, children and adults, who shaped my view of the world and provided me with such a satisfying career.

Judy Foster

# 1

# SOCIAL WORK – THE MODERN ERA

## WHY DO WE NEED SOCIAL WORKERS?

Despite the growth in prosperity over the decades, the need for social workers has not diminished. Many people from all walks of life need someone to approach at a time of trouble who is knowledgeable on different avenues of help and resources.

Social workers work with people in difficulty, whose lives have been thrown into disarray through poverty, accident or illness. They help families to cope, encouraging a nurturing structure for children and individuals to live fulfilling lives, despite physical, emotional or mental difficulties. Others may have difficulty fitting in with people through personal problems or borderline personality disorders due to neglect in infancy. These disorders can lead to conflict with those in authority, drug and alcohol abuse, family problems and difficulty in giving consistent affection. Social work departments often act like a fire blanket to protect the local community from the full impact of some of the troubled and troublesome people in their neighbourhood.

The Social Work Task Force[1] noted:

> Social work helps adults and children to be safe so they can cope and take control of their lives again. Social workers make life better for people in crisis who are struggling to cope, feel alone and cannot sort out their problems unaided:

- caring for family members
- having problems with family relationships and conflict
- struggling with challenges of growing old
- suffering serious personal troubles and mental distress
- having drug and alcohol problems
- facing difficulties as a result of disability
- being isolated within the community
- having practical problems with money or housing.

### A fledgling social worker

At the age of 23 in 1968, I heard a radio programme that described the work of child care officers and the way they helped children settle into foster homes for temporary periods. 'Wow what a brilliant thing to do!' I thought, and set about becoming one. Having had a dozen homes by the age of 13 (my father was a soldier), I instinctively wanted to help other children over these complex transitions. There was no hint that the position of social work in our society would change so much over 40 years that I would spend half my career in a profession battered by the media and blamed by everyone else.

In the 1960s, the Home Office had a drive to increase the number of child care social workers by setting up emergency courses for mature students under the guidance of Clare Winnicott. That was how I entered social work. There was considerable focus on the social sciences, human growth and development, the psychodynamics of families, skills in communicating with children and the legal framework – as well as the opportunity through supervision and group discussions to develop self-awareness and insight. This encouraged a reflective view that became part of my professional approach. On qualifying, the focus of my work was to develop relationships with children in social services care, families in need and with young offenders living in the community.

---

## The cases waiting for me

- I met William,[2] a two-year-old in a residential nursery, over a tube of pastilles. After discussing our favourites, he picked out all the blackcurrant ones for me. What an overture of friendship! No wonder I saw him through thick and thin over the following years.
- I was shocked to find Susan aged nine and Tim aged six living with a housemother in a small group home just because they no longer suited their mother's new life. Their little sister June, prone to fits, was in a nursery on the coast 70 miles away.
- Maggie had run off to the Isle of Wight festival aged 14 – 'What spirit', I thought, though my supervisor suspected some underlying envy in my reaction. I kept close by while she completed school, found a job, moved to lodgings, and had rows and reconciliations with her mum – teenage life in the round. Aged 17, she shyly told me of her affair with a well-known pop star. Fortunately my continued ignorance of the pop scene reassured her that I was a safe confidant.

---

### Finding substitute families

I supported foster carers and house mothers in their affectionate care of the children, and tried to return the children home, or find adoptive families or more accommodating placements. As Olive Stevenson[3] pointed out, our activities were both practical and thoughtful, designed to mitigate the trauma of separation as explored by John Bowlby[4] and also James and Joyce Robertson, lambasted for filming the acute distress of 'A two year old goes to hospital'.[5]

---

## Mark – a young blind boy, fostered then adopted

A young couple rang the bell of a boarding school for blind children, where they were introduced to a 10-year-old in my charge, called Mark, who needed a permanent loving home. His mother had been very young and unable to bring him back to the family home after his birth. It was an immense challenge for them. But they had the idealism, imagination and energy to create the right environment in which he could grow and develop affectionate relationships and the skills to lead an independent adult life.

During two years of fostering, they persuaded the headmaster of the local comprehensive to take Mark. Other pupils helped him to fit in. He took up music and played in the school band. Then they successfully adopted Mark. Years later we met by chance on the train. He was oblivious to the crowd around and immediately asked me about his mother.

I was shocked how deeply linked we must have always been in his mind. I realised again that the past cannot be wiped away, we can only try to understand it.

I built up shared experiences with children in care so we had a trusting relationship to work with when their lives next went pear-shaped. They used the unthreatening neutral space of a car journey or meal to share their confused, sad or angry feelings. As urged by Clare Winnicott,[6] this helped them to stay emotionally alive and maintain the capacity to feel – essential while efforts were made to rehabilitate them with their families, or to construct a separate life with the support of house mothers or foster carers. I also developed a good rapport with the police while spending many hours in the juvenile courts.

### The Seebohm reorganisation

The welfare services in the post-war period were fragmented and administered by a range of government departments such as Health, Education and the Home Office. Services were limited to protection from destitution rather than care of the whole person. However, all this changed with the Seebohm Report[7] in 1968, which reviewed the organisation and responsibilities of local authority personal social services.

The Seebohm reforms were implemented in 1971, combined with the introduction of generic practice and an emphasis on community well-being and citizenship. This structural modernisation of social work brought together the welfare, mental welfare and children's departments. It introduced a single social service department in local government providing a community-based and family-orientated service, headed by a qualified director. Social workers varied in background from the more practical welfare officers – who supported older people and those with physical disabilities in the community – to relationship-focused child care officers and mental welfare officers, and to psycho-dynamically orientated psychiatric social workers.

### Local branch of the British Association of Social Workers (BASW)

In 1972 I helped to set up a local branch of BASW, the new combined professional body for social workers. Our launch event focused on the new social services departments and Lord Seebohm was our first speaker. He said he had wanted to provide a single door for all the needy people to walk through so that clients would no longer be shunted from one department to another.

Another intention had been to increase the bargaining power of 'welfare' to equal or supersede that of the housing departments in local authorities – then the big spenders

*(continued)*

*(continued)*

(hence the current concerns having 'children in need' funds sharing the schools budget). Apparently Lord Seebohm had been taken completely by surprise to learn of the move to generic social work which had already been introduced into practice and into the new Certificate of Qualification in Social Work (CQSW). That major change had never been anticipated in his review.

These structural changes encouraged an expanded and radicalised young workforce to develop visions of social equality and social justice. Social work moved toward a community development model of innovative outreach schemes for all client groups.

### Managing an intake team in an inner city borough

I started work in a lively inner city borough as a student. The councillors decided to implement the required restructuring during my time there. This caused considerable turmoil and I was fortunate after qualifying to be given a permanent post. Social workers ran drop-in centres for the mentally ill, support groups for young mothers, neighbourhood warden schemes for the housebound, and diversion schemes for youngsters in trouble. We wanted to become more accessible, and held sessions in GP surgeries and clinics as well as having a stall at the local market.

I was concerned by the ad hoc management of new referrals to the office as the staff group expanded (with overflowing baskets of referral papers balanced on windowsills and worse). I pressed for a better system. Intake teams had been recommended by the National Institute of Social Work to meet generic community needs, and on promotion in 1973 I was asked to set one up. An experienced group of social workers dealt with all new referrals – providing assessments, undertaking short-term work and managing the boundary of the area team. I received expert supervision and support from my area manager and experienced members of staff, and did my best to provide the same, helped by a course on supervision. We also had access to consultancy at the local child guidance clinic.

### My first director of social services

Following the Seebohm reorganisation, we had our first director of social services. He introduced a modern leadership style, starting with calling everyone by their first name – unusual at the time. He set up a representatives group from each area team – as well as being valuable for staff, he could cannily keep tabs on staff views and issues.

He also 'walked the walk'. When duty senior late one Christmas Eve, I heard my colleague speak kindly on the phone saying 'I'm so sorry but that address is in Area 2, you will need to contact them – here's their number', then telling me of the homeless old man at the other end. The director had to own up that he had been testing the duty system!

I had to jump in the deep end and learn how to manage a team. We made mistakes but morale was high. I acted as a role model to new staff in my interactions with service users. It is disappointing, over 40 years later, that new first-line managers are still not offered routine management training before starting. I learnt the importance of good administration and filing systems, and minuted team meetings with agreed action points. I encouraged debate and reflective thinking, both in our allocation meetings and informal discussion and supervision. There was more paper recording as IT had not yet taken off. Nowadays investment in state-of-the-art IT is essential for busy social workers, ensuring proper records of service users' needs.

After the successful use of 'intake teams', a new approach was subsequently developed in my area office with a pilot 'patch' neighbourhood team on an isolated housing estate. Though resource intensive, this had the advantage of close community links, and was applied more widely.

## Closing institutions and supporting people to live in the community

There has been a revolution of social attitudes in the last 40 years in favour of supporting people to live independently in the community rather than in long-stay institutions. The press exposed the dire conditions in several isolated hospitals, such as the Ely Hospital[8] for mentally handicapped residents. In 1971 one of the first tasks of my new department was to manage the closure of a large 'Rowton House' in the centre of the borough. It provided temporary accommodation for 800 homeless men – reminiscent of George Orwell's *Down and Out in Paris and London*. We established hostels run by St Mungo's and The Cyrenians to support a number of men still in the borough after the closure.

During the next two decades, many large older residential institutions were closed. Group homes for people with learning disabilities or severe physical disabilities were set up. The development of anti-psychotic drugs freed thousands of long-term mental patients to live in sheltered accommodation in the community. Hostels were partly funded by selling off the original buildings. The provision of support in the community has been effective for people in mental distress, and for assessment of their needs for emergency treatment.

---

### Ron – who had lived in a large psychiatric institution

Ron had spent much of his adult life in such an institution, and subsequently enjoyed the freedom and support available in an inner city hostel. But this required more resources, such as weekly visits from a social worker to keep him on an even keel, and management links with the hostel staff to maintain morale. Ron was inclined to shout when people failed to understand him, and he was ejected by a neighbouring social work office for threatening behaviour.

He came down to our team for help. I asked an experienced colleague in mental health to meet Ron. He recommended that Ron had his own trainee social worker, Sally, whom he could meet every week. With this support, he flourished in the community. He came to the office with a bunch of tulips for Sally on her birthday. The memory is still heart-warming.

---

There is rarely justification to place someone with learning disabilities in hospital. Such people are not ill, but they are vulnerable to ill-treatment and exploitation. Social workers' support for people with learning disabilities and/or severe physical limitations has been life-changing to help them lead 'an ordinary life' with the aid of the Disability Living Allowance. There was considerable concern when it was proposed in 2016 that the allowance should be cut back, and the government backed down.

Mencap[9] pointed out in 2001 that there were 40,000 profoundly sensory handicapped children being cared for at home, often with inadequate support. The institutions may have gone, but society still fails to provide support for the families who have to look after their adult offspring, or enough small homes for group care. For example, I was struck by the care being taken at St Anne's Community Services[10] for each resident to undertake an ordinary task (e.g. when I visited, three were going shopping, two were preparing lunch and two were going swimming).

Stephen Hawking, the physicist, is severely physically limited by muscular dystrophy but gave the Reith lectures in 2016. The triumph of such determined people over adversity is gradually changing the attitude of the public toward physical disabilities.

---

### Ruby – a trainer and service user with physical disabilities

I met Ruby when setting up a national conference[11] on service user participation in social work education She and her visually impaired colleague had agreed to chair the conference. She was at home with her carer. She had a slight physique and lay on a trolley bed with headrest and microphone, raising her head for short periods. Ruby had a law degree and had set up her consulting business five years earlier. Her van was kitted out to meet her needs. She had already arranged overnight accommodation with her carers in a sympathetic environment. We discussed the organisation of the day and the speakers.

No one present will forget the impact of this delicate figure in charge of our agenda. She confronted us all with her individuality and humanity. I remember my despair when these same colleagues avoided the workshops led by service users, instead crowding in to the leading professor's room. Ruby calmed my tears of anger and embarrassment. She explained that this often happened. It was because people were frightened, and she understood this – 'So pushing them out of the window wouldn't really help, would it?'

---

### Training and development

If you are in social work for the long haul, continuous learning is essential to keep up to date on the latest thinking and practice. When I was offered, in my thirties, the role of managing and teaching on the department's trainee social worker scheme, I undertook a master's degree at Brunel University in public and social administration. This provided valuable understanding of management in different organisations – and insight into the 'surface issues' of social work that could help or hinder working practices. My supervisor[12] for the dissertation stressed the value of supervision and its psychoanalytic underpinning structure.

Wanting to learn more about the unconscious – or 'depth' – issues in groups and organisations, I studied at the Tavistock Clinic on the advanced course in consultation to organisations, groups and individuals. This provided helpful insight for my role in leading a section which supported all the teams of the organisation. More recently I completed a doctorate in social work there,[13] the research of which underpins part of this book.

Social services departments received training grants directly from government, and had the capacity to run programmes to assist staff with the implementation of new policies. We were familiar with the strengths and weaknesses of the teams across the department, their relative effectiveness, and the challenges facing each fieldwork team, day care establishment and residential home. I encouraged others to develop consultancy skills, which we offered to staff groups across the department and to the senior management team. We worked hard to put into practice the ideas in some key text books[14] on the impact of our early experience on both learning and teaching. During these years, my team earned the sobriquet of 'being the oil in the joints of the department'.[15]

---

### My experience as a training manager

As a manager of an in-house training and development section in a social services department, I was able to help the organisation provide a better containing space to support all staff in their different roles. I became job-share training manager for five years – thanks to the local council's equal opportunities policy and the determination of my senior managers. It was a bit disappointing to read 30 years later of two candidates barred from applying together to be a job-share Member of Parliament.

---

### The commissioner–provider reorganisation

When the commissioner/provider split was introduced into social services departments in the early 1990s, the Central Council for Education and Training in Social Work (CCETSW) was developing training standards and implementation guidance on national vocational qualifications. I joined to improve residential child care standards, mentoring skills and service user involvement.

Competitive tendering has transformed how social care is delivered,[16] with the benefit of more choice for service users from the voluntary and private sectors. Improvement in support in social care is seen as the responsibility of providers, with guidance from the Social Care Institute for Excellence and Skills for Care.

However, the implementation required a complex administrative structure for social workers to commission services from competing providers – with commissioners, providers, inspectors and auditors, etc. Assessments often produced more issues. There are difficulties in inspecting and auditing the provision of the commissioned services, particularly now the 'for profit' sector is a major provider (e.g. for children's services). Eight commercial fostering agencies made over £40 million profit in 2014–15[17] from providing foster placements to local authorities. Commercial agencies will argue they have improved the quality of foster care, but it is also arguable that charities and effective local authorities are equally adept at doing this – and do not take millions of pounds in profits.

---

### Mental health standards

When CCETSW was wound up in 2000, I joined Topss England,[18] which later became 'Skills for Care', to develop mental health training standards. These were intended to form a bridge between the medical and social care approaches to mental distress. Research[19] found that service users with severe mental health problems living in the community preferred to be monitored by a social worker rather than a community psychiatric nurse. However, mental health social workers were still seconded from their local authorities to 'integrated mental health trusts'.

Further changes have occurred in the training of mental health professionals. The role of the approved social worker[20] (ASW) was replaced in 2007 by the approved mental health professional (AMHP), which can be undertaken by other professionals such as community psychiatric nurses after appropriate training.

---

## Continuous learning for mental health professionals

A small group of us set up the Social Perspectives Network to stimulate debate on ways to keep the social viewpoint in modern mental health services. This network was used creatively by service users, academic colleagues, social workers, voluntary organisations and central government policy makers.

Given five years' funding from the Department of Health, we provided continuous learning opportunities through regular workshops, and published detailed reports[21] on different aspects of the subject. Two colleagues published useful books[22] for practitioners and students. When formal funding ended, the website and annual meetings were maintained by some of the group for another decade.

---

The government initiative on social work for better mental health[23] was a welcome announcement by the Chief Social Worker for Adults in January 2016. This aimed to clarify the specific roles of mental health social workers within the joint trusts, which were formed in 2000. This initiative links with the launch of Think Ahead,[24] a new graduate entry programme, in 2015 for those wanting to be social workers in mental health.

---

## Some emergency calls had their funny side

- One winter evening, the GP and I arrived at an address to find the place was in darkness. The unwell man had taken out all the electrical wiring and window frames to stop the voices getting at him, an action his wife thought perfectly sensible. We were sitting on boxes in the gloom when a head popped through the gaping window saying 'Paraffin anyone?' – the vendor for paraffin heaters on his weekly round! We all agreed to postpone any further assessment until the morning.
- In the 1970s there were a large number of squatters in the small houses in the streets around our offices. One duty call involved negotiating with a prestigious hospital to agree to a home birth for a hippy mother. As there was no electricity, it would be by candlelight. The hospital team thought she must be mad to consider this. After a risk assessment of the home and the mother-to-be, the team agreed with us that compulsory admission under the Mental Health Act was rather excessive, but they would bring emergency lighting for the birth.

## Financial resources

The austerity cuts of 2013–16 led to plummeting resources for local authorities and their charitable providers. This put at risk community support and provider organisations, such as small charities providing residential accommodation for the mentally ill. New forms of ring-fenced money have been announced from time to time, but sooner or later cuts to other forms of support have adversely affected the poor – for example, by cutting housing benefit which penalises people with an extra bedroom but providing no alternative accommodation, or declaring people with a recognised mental health problem to be fit for work and removing their Disability Living Allowance.

---

### Preventive work: keeping young dads involved with their children

I was chair of St Michael's Fellowship,[25] a charity working with very young parents in a deprived multi-racial part of an inner city, helping them to keep in touch with their children and out of gangs. We employed a youth worker to 'collect dads', looking out for teenage young men with their girlfriends in the antenatal clinic and telling them about a weekly dads-to-be group held in a local pub. It proved a welcome support. The young men gradually understood what their girlfriends were going through, learnt to support the mums-to-be, and often witnessed their babies being born.

Combined with a 'dads only' session at the local playground, and literacy classes to increase their chances of employment, the project extended its reach, and within two years over 150 children gained their fathers back in their lives. After ten successful years the scheme was curtailed in 2016 following further cuts in public spending.

---

There was wide publicity on the countrywide shortage of acute beds in the mental health trusts, and the limited funds for specialist treatment or supportive accommodation. In contrast there was surprisingly little objection to the withdrawal of the Education Maintenance Allowance, which covered travel fares to tertiary college for the over 16s. This may appear insignificant but it was a body blow for impoverished young people. In addition, local authorities could not afford to engage care assistants for long enough to wash, dress and feed older people at home.

---

### Sure Start and St Michael's Fellowship – effect of financial cuts

When supportive services were offered through Sure Start programmes at children's centres in the early 2000s, I cheered that support would at last reach those in need. For example 'cook up' sessions were held where mums, staff and children shared the healthy cheap meals that the adults cooked. The charity St Michael's Fellowship provided these popular courses, including one on domestic violence for very young mums. But financial cuts in 2016 meant the centres could no longer afford to engage them.

---

The government's stated policy is to devolve more funding responsibility for municipal services from Whitehall to local councils.[26] Councils have been given powers to raise extra funding for adult social care through a local social care council tax, along with a £1.5 billion Better Care fund to enable closer working with the NHS. However, this is against a financial environment of massive cuts to local authorities. Local authorities are working hard to preserve their social services but this is a challenge.

## The inquiries into child protection tragedies

Neglect and occasional ill-treatment in the family was part of life for the poor prior to the Second World War and lingered on through the 1950s and 1960s. But then hospitals started to become more aware of maltreatment. As an auxiliary on a children's ward in 1967, I took part in a discussion with the doctors on whether a badly bruised toddler on the ward, said to have fallen downstairs, was in fact a victim of the newly defined 'battered baby syndrome'.

In those first years we had remarkably few cases presented as child abuse inquiries, probably because children at risk were more frequently already received into care. My team had a handful of requests for place of safety orders. Occasionally the family psychiatrist at the local hospital would ask for a place of safety order on a Friday afternoon 'just in case the parents discharge their baby over the weekend' as he had upset them and was worried.

But the first child protection investigation in our office followed the publication of the Maria Colwell[27] Report. This put responsibility for preventing child abuse and child deaths firmly on social workers, without any of the previous structural anonymity.[28] A steady stream of child death inquiries throughout the 1980s and 1990s increased the resources needed to investigate allegations of abuse. This was at the expense of preventive work with families.

Inquiry reports (of which there have been 70 in the last 40 years) have tended to focus on the need for stricter procedures, which have not necessarily helped effective practice. The media's vitriolic reporting of child deaths, due to lack of protection – about 150 a year[29] – contrasts with its relative silence on avoidable hospital deaths, around 9,000 per year.[30] Malcolm Dean commented on this contrast:

> Social workers have to tread a perilous path along which on one side they will be damned for taking children away from their families without good cause, and on the other for failing to take away children who were at serious risk of harm.

The Victoria Climbié report[31] brought about an investigation of social work performance by Lord Laming. He recommended a range of procedural changes, as well as the transfer of responsibility for social work with children and families from the Department of Health to the Department for Education. The public outrage at the death of Peter Connelly in November 2007, in the same borough in which Victoria Climbié died in 2000, led to the Secretary of State for Education[32] at a press conference directing Haringey Council to sack its director of children's services without even a chance to respond to the Ofsted report. This marked a nadir of public confidence in social work.

The Social Work Task Force was set up to identify the main problems in 2009, followed by the Social Work Reform Board which carried out the Task Force's recommendations to improve social work training and practice. The Reform Board was disbanded in 2013 when the Office of Chief Social Worker was set up. Eileen Munro[33] led a review on better ways of handling child protection, which reported in 2011. The Child Protection Task Force,[34] set up in 2015, based its objectives on her report with emphasis on supporting social work practice and leadership.

## Strong leadership needed to tackle the blame culture

The profession needs leaders as role models for staff at all levels – and also leaders able to represent the profession, to stick up for social workers, and to put over to the public and politicians the tough issues facing social workers when they are working in very challenging circumstances. The much greater scrutiny by the media of problematic and tragic cases in recent years has led to a blame culture. Encouraged by the popular press, society tends to be ambivalent about users of social services, often seeing them as undeserving misfits, with social workers blamed for any problems arising.

There is a tendency to put the best possible gloss on a difficult situation and hope the media attention will go away, rather than explain upfront to the public the tricky dilemmas being addressed. Social services managers in Haringey during the Climbié tragedy were criticised for trying to hold back documents in order to limit inadequacies in children's services being highlighted in the inquiry.[35] Investigations into tragedies look in detail at the external actions of social workers from an administrative and legal perspective. One hears the comment 'It must never happen again' with sinking heart. Human beings are fallible, and clients are often manipulative. Current policies try to construct safer systems, but care is needed that these are not so complex and time consuming to operate that new risks arise.

The profession lost a centralising hub when the CCETSW was abolished in 2000. We had expected the College of Social Work[36] to provide leadership across the social work profession. It was a sad day when the government withdrew its funding. It is important that an alternative for this role is developed with involvement of the profession. Membership should be encouraged by, for example, being made mandatory on registration. The decision by the government in 2016 to change the professional regulator after three years and to establish a new regulator in 2018 caused disquiet in the profession.

The setting up of the Office of Chief Social Worker in 2013, and the appointment of two Chief Social Workers (one for adults and the other for children and families) is a step in the right direction to provide leadership and consistency in national policies. But this will require effective co-ordination between the Department of Health and the Department for Education. Otherwise there is the risk of inconsistent initiatives (e.g. for social work education straddling children and adults).

The focus of the NHS and Community Care Act 1990 was on the assessment of the excluded for services, treatment or intervention – along with greater inspection and regulation, rather than help for the excluded to re-engage with their community through a relationship with the social worker. Hence the emphasis in the Care Act 2014 on service users' and carers' well-being[37] is an encouraging development. It also sets out a clear legal framework for how local authorities should protect adults at risk of abuse or neglect by establishing safeguarding adults boards, with membership including the local authority, NHS and police.

---

### Example of the intention of the Care Act 2014 being anticipated

Much of the work of social workers is confidential. A locum GP told me that she applauded the professionalism of her local ASWs[38] who would traipse into the woods to check on a tent-dwelling hermit. When I suggested that she put her appreciation in a letter, she cited confidentiality concerns. Hence this type of good news story remains unknown.

---

The 'Knowledge and Skills Statement for Social Workers in Adult Services'[39] is particularly useful while the new Care Act 2014 is implemented, and social workers get to grips with their new role of advising people on their needs and well-being rather than assessing appropriateness for services. The statement notes that:

> Social workers should enable people to experience personalised, integrated care and support them to maintain their independence and well-being, cope with change, attain the outcomes they want and need, understand and manage risk, and participate in the life of their communities.

A named social worker will be valuable for everyone with a learning disability, autism and a mental health condition, although the role will need clear definition. This should help this group to live an ordinary life rather than being considered a medical problem or lost in the community. In addition the Chief Social Worker for Children has announced far reaching reforms across children's services, which are under discussion.[40] The knowledge and skills required by approved child and family practitioners have been agreed – as well as for accredited practice leaders and supervisors.[41]

### My research study of three fieldwork teams

Inquiries into child deaths have set out much about the failing organisations in which the events took place. The lack of careful reflection before taking appropriate action has been frequently pointed out. The Victoria Climbié Inquiry listed a catalogue of administrative and organisational failings – a toxic backdrop to a series of poor decisions. The media made much of the missed chances and errors of the social workers.

I wanted to find out whether these criticisms implied a change in the quality of social work practice compared to my experience as a manager or reflected a much tougher case load and operating environment. I decided to study front-line teams and see for myself how they were faring. This included both social workers' relationships with service users and social services organisations themselves. So I spent several months with three different fieldwork teams in an inner city to see how effectively they used their time and professional skills to deliver the services required – and the quality of their supporting environment. This is set out in Chapters 4 onwards. Case examples from the three teams are also used to illustrate points in Chapters 2 and 3.

## Comment

Much of this chapter is based on my personal experience. A great deal has changed in social work practice, but my strong belief from teaching is that the new cohort of social workers are as able and committed as we were in the early 1970s. But they are operating in a much more complex and challenging environment of media attention, blame, regulation, tight financial resources, increasing numbers of service users and heavy overload. There were over 600,000 support requests[42] in 2014–15 for local authority adult social care services, which resulted in the provision of short- or long-term support. There have also been increasing demands on child protection services - see page 126. The demand is rising with more complex care requirements putting more pressures on stretched social workers. Hence the job has become a lot tougher, and society needs to give them full backing with the necessary resources.

## Notes

1 Building a safe, confident future – The final report of the Social Work Task Force. 2009
2 All names of social workers and service users throughout this book have been changed and anonymised.
3 Stevenson, O. 1998. 'It was more difficult than we thought'. *Children and Family Social Work* 3: 158–161.
4 Bowlby, J. 1953. *Child care and the growth of love*. Penguin Books.
5 Robertson, J. and Robertson, J. 1952. 'A two year old goes to hospital'. Robertson Films.
6 Winnicott, C. 1968. 'Communicating with children'. In: R. Tod (ed.), *Disturbed children*. London: Longmans.
7 Seebohm Report 1968. Report of the Committee on Local Authority and Allied Personal Social Services. Cmnd 3703. The committee was appointed in 1965 'to review the organisation and responsibilities of local authority personal social services in England and Wales, and to consider desirable changes to secure an effective family service'.
8 Report of the Committee of Inquiry into allegations of ill-treatment of patients and other irregularities at the Ely Hospital, Cardiff. March 1969. Cmnd 3975.
9 Mencap. 2001. 'No Ordinary Life'. www.mencap.org.uk
10 St Anne's Community Services in Yorkshire and Northumberland. www.st-annes.org.uk
11 Central Council of Education and Training in Social Work (CCETSW) conference 1998.
12 Barker, M. 1982. 'Through experience towards theory: a psychodynamic contribution to social work education'. *Social Work Education* 2(1): 3–25.
13 Foster, J. 'Thinking on the front line – why some social work teams struggle and others thrive'. Thesis for Doctorate in Social Work. http://drjudyfoster.blogspot.co.uk
14 Knowles, M. 1973. *The adult learner – a neglected species*. 2nd edn. Houston: Gulf; Salzberger-Wittenberg, E., Henry, G. and Osborne, E. 1983. *The emotional experience of learning and teaching*. London: Routledge.
15 Social Services Inspectorate 1993.
16 *The Guardian*. 17 August 2015. 'Why do social care providers get less support than their NHS counterparts?'
17 *The Guardian*. 11 January 2016. 'Why do we let fostering agencies profit from caring for vulnerable children?'
18 Topss England – the national training organisation for the personal social services.
19 MacDonald, G. and Sheldon, B. 1997. 'Community care services for the mentally ill: consumers' views'. *International Journal of Social Psychiatry* 43(1): 35–55.
20 My study of the three teams was carried out before this change and hence refers to ASWs.
21 Available for download at www.spn.org.uk

22  Tew, J. (ed.). 2004. *Social perspectives in mental health: developing social models to understand and work with mental distress.* London: Jessica Kingsley; Gilbert, P. 2003. *The value of everything.* Lyme Regis: Russell House Publishing.

23  Department of Health. January 2016. 'Social work for better mental health – a strategic statement'.

24  http://thinkahead.org/

25  www.stmichaelsfellowship.org.uk

26  *The Guardian.* 17 December 2015. 'Councils face billions more in budget cuts from April'.

27  Department of Health. 1974. 'Report of Committee of Inquiry into the care and supervision provided in relation to Maria Colwell'. London: HMSO.

28  Waddell, M. 1989. *Living in two worlds: psychodynamic theory and social work practice.* Free Associations.

29  Dean, M. 2012. *Democracy under attack.* Policy Press. pp. 312–313.

30  *The Guardian.* 6 July 2015. 'Study finds 750 avoidable deaths a month in NHS hospitals'.

31  Report by Lord Laming on the Victoria Climbié Inquiry – CM5730. January 2003.

32  *The Guardian.* 29 October 2013. 'Ed Balls no regrets about sacking Sharon Shoesmith over Baby P affair'.

33  Department for Education. May 2011. 'The Munro review of child protection'. CM8062.

34  Press release from Prime Minister's Office. 24 June 2015. 'New taskforce to transform child protection'.

35  *The Guardian.* 4 February 2002. 'Key figures in the Climbié case'.

36  College of Social Work established in 2011, and funding withdrawn in June 2015.

37  *The Guardian.* 5 June 2014. 'What are the important changes to the Care Act?'

38  Approved Social Workers.

39  Department of Health. March 2015. 'Knowledge and skills statement for social workers in adult services'.

40  Speech by Secretary of State for Education – January 2016.

41  Department for Education. November 2015. 'Knowledge and skills statements for practice leaders and practice supervisors'.

42  Department of Health. Annual Report by the Chief Social Worker for Adults 2015–16.

# 2

# SUPPORT FOR DIFFERENT
# SERVICE USERS

This chapter describes three types of support – empowerment, maintenance and containment – and considers the service users who can benefit from these. The difficulty of providing support for some service users is recognised (e.g. those at risk of abuse, with personality disorders or brain damage).

Two pointers to good social work practice ring true across the decades. First, Eileen Younghusband[1] considered that social work can help service users 'make a better go of it with themselves and others and have a bit more elbow room in their social circumstances'. Even quite small adjustments can make a significant difference to an individual – for example, access to a chiropody service can allow him to walk to the shops and reduce his sense of isolation. I learnt so much from the occupational therapist in the office on what to look out for when visiting older people at home. A half-day training should be part of everyone's knowhow (e.g. the difficulties with low chairs, risks with dangerous mats, poor lighting, trailing wires, kitchens, bathroom grab rails, etc.).

Second, Donald Winnicott[2] told the Association of Social Workers in 1965 that social work 'counteracts the disintegrating forces in individuals, families and local social groups'. This was a rallying call to social workers not to give in to the negative forces in society. This determination is still present in every healthy social work office, protecting and working with vulnerable clients. As in Jill's tale (page 39), social workers need to look at the different points of view in any family situation, and decide which matters most. Marlene (page 94) supported her client against the housing department, the police and the medical profession, and found a good outcome for all.

Social workers need to be perceptive, curious to the client's real needs, interested in the person behind the problem, and good organisers. They are effective when they make accurate assessments of needs, and provide services to meet them; have knowledge of local resources relevant for the client; and provide counselling and ongoing support when necessary.[3] A mental health service user told a working group that his social worker understood his earlier family problems. He felt she was interested in him, and not just his illness.

---

**Understanding why a client was suicidal**

A colleague, a manager in a community mental health team, was short staffed so she had to provide the client's medication instead of the community psychiatric nurse. She was surprised to meet a young man at home who had recently made a serious

*(continued)*

---

*(continued)*

suicide attempt. In conversation she asked what had driven him to such drastic action. He explained that he had just been diagnosed HIV positive. His need for reassurance and information needed to be met – and not necessarily with doses of strong drugs!

## EMPOWERMENT, MAINTENANCE, CONTAINMENT

### Empowerment

Each team worked with slightly different groups of vulnerable adults. Each had varied characteristics. Most of the District Team's work was focused on 'empowerment', the public agenda of social work with its offer of hope, transformation and personalisation for the service user. This gives a sense of practical and emotional betterment, and an easing of hostile landscapes. In this relationship, a service user's necessary dependence, provoked by troublesome life events or ill health, meets an empathetic response from the social worker and from society. The social worker supplies the necessary ego support for the service user to bring about change, along with practical knowledge to access resources.

---

### Valerie – empowering a client after a stroke

'I had one couple where the husband had a stroke just after they were married. He was unsteady on his feet and had little strength in his left arm. His wife was always anxious, saying he had frequent falls and often rang the ambulance to collect him. She wanted him to move to residential care. I told her he couldn't go there as he could still do his personal care – but she did not believe he could cope.

He eventually agreed to go into sheltered accommodation if available. He was given a place in the borough but then said he wanted a motor scooter. I didn't think he could manage one but he bought it anyway. Last month I was up in town and saw this person riding towards me and I thought "I know that man – and it was him!"

If I had believed his wife rather than listening to him, he would have ended up in a residential home and all his skills would have gone. He then booked a holiday, arranged all the transport and took himself off. Although the staff were quite concerned, he had a great time. I was really pleased for this gentleman. This is a success however you look at it!'

---

### Maintenance

Those vulnerable people who need physical care, often permanently, were evident in the Hospital Team and the District Team. I use the term 'maintenance' to describe the care they were expected to receive – that is to help maintain the skills they still possessed.[4] The requirements of meeting the discharge legislation reduced the social workers' freedom to reach an independent decision. At times they felt ethically conflicted. There is a major responsibility in helping these vulnerable service users to maintain or regain the individuality that is easily lost in an institutional environment. The specialist team for the homeless mentally ill was successful in placing many of its clients in supportive hostels.

---

### Sheila – maintaining support for a client with cerebral palsy

Sheila worked in the District Team, reviewing all the out-of-borough placements for the under 65s. Clive aged 50 had cerebral palsy and lived in a sheltered home in Wales, run by a charity. Sheila had visited every six months in recent years and knew him well.

Clive's parents had been relieved to see him happily settled, and to know before they died that he was safe and his future was secure. He had a voluntary job helping twice a week in the local library. He and a friend from the hostel were also regulars at the local pub, enjoying the company and quizzes.

Then the charity dropped a bombshell. It would no longer provide homes for adults with cerebral palsy. Everyone in the hostel would be made homeless. The local council would house those in the borough – but the rest were likely to be evicted for their home authorities to sort out. Clive was terrified that he might have to move back to his parents' borough which he had left as a teenager and where he knew no one.

Fortunately his friend's sister advocated for both Clive and his friend to stay within the area where he had lived for over 20 years. Sheila was supportive with long-distance calls and visits. She and her manager visited, and were able to reach a deal with the local authority to continue to house Clive while the home authority paid. Whew – and no thanks to the charity!

---

## Containment

The third intervention, I call 'containment' – when the behaviour of service users extends from the erratic and demanding, which was fairly common in the District Team, in patients with dementia or Alzheimer's in the hospital, to acute or chronic mental distress and psychosis covered by the Mental Health Team. The term 'containment' may imply more passivity than is meant – help for distressed and difficult people to sustain relationships with those who can affect their circumstances is a demanding and active process. These service users, living with chronic and ingrained problems, needed longer timescales of supportive intervention to effect any change in their approach to dealing with life's problems.

Following on from a successful pilot study 'Reaching out: think family', the government set up the Troubled Families Programme in 2012. Local authorities applied for funding for families where no adult was in work, children were not in school, and family members were involved in crime or antisocial behaviour – our old 'problem families' of the past. Additionally domestic violence, relationship issues and mental and physical health problems would often be present. The intention was to 'turn round' 120,000 troubled families across England in three years. Some key improvements were being measured in the families. Unfortunately, as some leave the programme 'cured', other welfare cuts are pushing more families into this category.

## Mrs Y – providing containment for an agitated client

Mrs Y had asked the home carer to collect her children from school. The home care provider had rung the office for advice on a Friday afternoon. Leroy, the duty senior, told me that the office had commissioned an hour and a half's home care Monday to Friday to help her around the house. He rang Mrs Y and had a courteous but firm conversation with her. He explained that these carers were paid to help her in the house, and that they were not allowed to do child care tasks – only the carers from 'children and families' were authorised to do that.

Half an hour later, Sara, the administrator, leant over and said that Mrs Y had phoned back and cancelled the care service as she intended to commit suicide and would not need it. Leroy contacted her again, stressing that his service could not collect children. He was supportive but firm. She said she was going to kill herself and put the telephone down.

Leroy's discussion with Mrs Y reminded me of similar conversations that I had held in the past with 'problem families', when required to set boundaries in a reasonable and almost parental manner. It made me feel quite at home. His calm manner on the telephone suggested Mrs Y was well known to the team. She might have been one of a number of service users who easily became angry or hysterical at the unexpected or in order to get her way.

The home care provider rang an hour later to say Mrs Y had left the house to collect the children. The carer, who had been there for the hour and a half, did not know whether to leave. Leroy advised that the carer should write a note and also return on Monday as Mrs Y was rather volatile and not good at thinking.

Mrs Y did not fare well with her social work contact. She had been told the following Monday both by the District Team and the children's team that she needed to contact the other, so had rung back in understandable confusion. Rich, another administrator, tried to find out how to amend the contract with the care providers. He discovered that as her carers were paid for by two departments, the departments needed to agree which was the lead agency. The lead agency would then have the power to alter the contract. Until they had agreed that – although it was unclear who 'they' were – nothing could be done. Like Mrs Y, I was left unsure if anyone was going to help unravel this Kafkaesque muddle.

Two months later I heard Yvonne, a social worker, ask Andy, the area manager, what she should do as her telephone conversation to reassess carer support for Mrs Y had gone badly. Should she visit to assess her need for home care? Andy suggested she should ask the care agency for feedback on any problems and asked 'She wasn't horrible to you, was she?' Yvonne replied that Mrs Y had tried to be.

I longed to champion Mrs Y's need for some face-to-face contact rather than the telephone calls, which she appeared to find so difficult. Her outbursts may have affected her reputation as staff seemed to be wary of an assessment, just like Leroy weeks earlier. The continued use of telephone calls seemed a defensive action to ward off involvement.

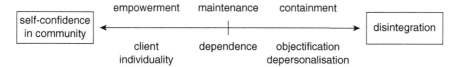

*Figure 2.1* Service users on independence–dependence spectrum

When planning an intervention with a client, the social worker has to assess in which areas the client needs help. While maximising independence for service users with physical or learning disabilities, the social worker may recommend more practical help with both 'maintenance' and 'containment' aspects.

## DIFFERENT SERVICE USER CONDITIONS

### The spectrum of service user dependency

Figure 2.1 illustrates the dynamic flow of a person's dependency needs from social engagement to depersonalisation – the way these change and increase with age, but also decrease for children as they grow and reach maturity. The horizontal axis represents independence–dependence, the service user's expressiveness and emotional situation. Service users who possess individuality and the ability to engage with others lie at the left of the axis; those with greater dependence around the middle; and those with loss of individuality lie to the right of the axis – where they risk being objectified by the system, and then depersonalised and at risk of abuse.

---

#### Mr J – mentally infirm and becoming depersonalised

The social workers in the Hospital Team worked with those who were often isolated, with no family, memory or social skills to express their individuality. At a multi-disciplinary team (MDT) meeting the staff nurse talked of Mr J – 'The nursing home wants him transferred'. 'They are usually pretty good. Why's that?' asked the social worker. 'He's fine in hospital but he's quite antisocial with them. He pees into cups and does other horrible things. So they want him to have an elderly mentally infirm assessment'. The risk for such vulnerable service users is that they become objectified and then depersonalised within the care system.

---

Vulnerability of service users can easily lead to exploitation and abuse. Social workers and others in the field (e.g. police, health workers, teachers) need support to have the inner confidence to recognise and think the unthinkable – and ask questions such as: 'Is this parent putting the vulnerable child's needs first, or are they exploiting or ill-treating them (e.g. sexual abuse in the family)?' There is considerable unconscious pressure to fall in line with the rest of society and believe that all is well. But we are appalled when a group sets up a vindictive witch hunt in response to an individual's tale (e.g. the abortive high-profile police investigation into claims of a Westminster paedophile ring on the basis of a single witness[5]).

## A social worker told me about attempted exploitation

'My client has a younger sister who didn't want to know them and was not interested in their life. That changed when my client was awarded £1.5 million in damages for birth injuries. All of a sudden this other sister came out of the woodwork and gave up her job to look after her sister and mother. She now has power of attorney. Both mum and daughter are asking how they can get rid of her. The sister is saying that they are both mad. They accuse her of trying to take the money and she wants them put away in a home'.

Society's ambivalence to dependence and long-term needs undermines the provision of support. Regrettably society values throughput and cure rather than support and marginal improvements. But social workers also require adequate support to understand and withstand the emotional and intellectual pain projected into them by these 'hard-to-reach' or psychologically damaged clients, while still exercising measured thought and judgement (as observed by Andrew Cooper[6]).

Service users in the District Team, though often dependent, were mainly able to engage the social workers in a joint project to maintain or improve their daily lives. They are shown at the left of the axis in Figure 2.1. Current policies for social workers to empower service users support this group well. However, cuts in the Disability Living Allowance in 2015 had damaging consequences for mentally ill service users and physically disabled people. Hospital service users were often at the maintenance/dependence stage with growing numbers deteriorating such as Mr J.

Being a specialist group, the team for the homeless mentally ill worked mostly with people with chronic symptoms. These service users needed long-term support, based on maintenance and containment. The team's major irritant was that sheltered hostels, which provided the right balance of support and independence, often limited a client's stay to two years when it was needed permanently. The local community mental health teams and their specialist groups took all other referrals, including people with anxiety, depression, schizophrenia and bipolar disorder.

## What is a borderline personality?

Children are likely to grow up into troubled and troubling people if they have had no containing adult to help them develop the ability to feel and think. They are likely to require the support or intervention of social welfare agencies. Lacking positive relationships in everyday life, they have no internalised good experiences inside themselves. Due to indifference, neglect or cruelty, the infant is denied a nurturing relationship with the mind of his care-giver, and therefore misses subsequent opportunities for developing a mature mental apparatus.

## A deprived mother without the internal resources to provide care

Jenny and I bonded when we spent two hours together in a traffic jam trying to reach a mother and baby hostel in the rush hour. We failed and Liam, her two-year-old boy, had to stay with an elderly foster carer. The mother was a waif-like girl, needy and impulsive. We sat over cups of tea while she described her ideal job – being a waitress in a café putting flowers on the tables and bringing lovely meals to the customers. Meanwhile it proved hard for her to make a home for them both – which was our shared loss.

The behaviours that make up the clinical syndrome of 'borderline personality'[7] are also recognisable in many service users – including impulsiveness, unstable but intense relationships, identity disturbances, mood instability, inappropriate and intense anger, frantic efforts to avoid abandonment, suicide threats, a feeling of emptiness and boredom.

Most service users with borderline personalities, through ill-treatment in infancy or from early trauma, have a serious problem in functioning in the world. They were typical of the mothers of my children in care and featured in the workload of all three teams. They cannot easily think through day-to-day events and relationships. A small proportion of such clients take a high proportion of social work time. People need to be able to use words and thoughts to sort through current and past anxieties. The Mental Health Team was structured to provide them with effective help, and the District Team also made considerable effort with such clients.

### Well-known clients thrown off a flight for drunken behaviour

When I asked interviewees to 'tell me about a case that is giving you grief', examples often came from confused and complex families, known to the social services for decades. Those with borderline characteristics were often mentioned. The national news was dominated once by a family of eight aged from 35 to 70. They had been thrown off a charter flight after an emergency landing due to drunken behaviour. They turned out to be well-known clients – a troubled family who had aged but not matured!

### Service users suffering from severe trauma

In her case studies on survivors of disasters, Caroline Garland[8] shows the devastating effect of severe trauma on an individual's mental apparatus. In a state of shock, the victims lose the ability to manage and contain their feelings, even losing the power of words. In the same way as a newborn infant, they try to manage the flood of terrifying images by projection on to those around them. This impacts on their ability to recover:

> Since the capacity for symbolisation (using words to represent a feeling or event), and for thinking 'about' something such as an event which itself is over, is a necessary part of working through – of dealing with, of laying to rest – a psychically painful experience.

---

**The value of words to banish post-traumatic stress disorder (PTSD)**

A few years ago there was a programme on Remembrance Day which included a veteran of the Korean War. He had been an 18-year-old conscript and spoke of the horror of the battlefield and his nightmares throughout his life. Then the previous year, a friend asked him to talk to the school cadet corps about his wartime experience. After some prevarication, he eventually agreed and prepared carefully for the talk, which was well received. To his astonishment, he had no nightmare that night or subsequently.

---

Garland points out similar assaults are made on an individual's mental structures if they are a victim of less dramatic though equally pernicious traumatic events. These can include physical or sexual abuse, abandonment by a parent, divorce, loss of employment, the death of a child, and other events. Many users of social care services have been such victims. For example, a psychiatrist friend conducted a small survey of patients on a female acute mental health ward. She was shocked that most had been sexually abused in the family as young girls. There is a danger that people who work with them can be unaware of or inured to the damage they have suffered.

## Service users who depend on others for their care

A large group of people who seek help from the social services have physical or mental frailties and are dependent on others for their personal care. Paul Hoggett notes that 'there is a deep-seated hatred of dependency within our culture which needs to be understood'.[9] This hatred, which disguises our deep fear of being dependent ourselves, can lead to dangerous outcomes – as shown by the abuse of young adults with learning disabilities in hospital care (e.g. at Winterbourne View[10]), or the murder of a vulnerable man in Bristol with learning disabilities who had sought help from the police.[11]

To avoid projecting this fear, we need to acknowledge our own needs. He adds:

> We all occasionally struggle not to be overwhelmed by feelings and, to the extent that we cannot find the inner resources to contain and give meaning to what we experience, we depend upon others. We depend upon them for reassurance and empathy, to show the strength and confidence in the future that we ourselves cannot at that moment find or just, simply, to be there, reliably and attentively, with us. We call this care, something all of us give and receive.

Social workers recognise the importance of providing a relationship, but also the importance of maintaining a boundary against the sometimes seemingly endless demands of the service user – being clear about the social worker's responsibility and that of the client. The introduction of care management in the 1990s brought about a diminution of the perceived relevance of the social work relationship. Cases are 'closed' after the first review as departments attempt to avoid long-term supportive commitments. However, the District Team successfully managed to provide a core of service users with 'good enough' long-term help.

---

### Patrick – able to live in the community with chronic schizophrenia

Patrick was a family friend whom we met every Sunday evening for a drink and meal for over ten years. He had a psychotic breakdown suddenly in his early thirties. After the initial shock and distress to his family and friends, he was fortunate in having the intellectual and financial resources to keep in regular employment between episodes. He gave me much good advice over the decades, such as 'They ought to give us psychotics key workers' and 'Next time I would like to stay at home, looked after by my key worker'. And why not? That came straight from the horse's mouth!

He relapsed regularly, but he then had a progressive illness to manage on top of this. His remaining family wanted the best for him and thought he should move into a residential home. But he was reluctant to do this. His social worker supported his view and found a regular carer for him. With that support and a simple routine, he continued to live in his own flat in the community.

---

## UNDERSTANDING SERVICE USERS

The next section explores psychological models that throw light on the behaviour of service users. A deeper understanding of service users requires exploration of family relationships and child development. The quality of childhood experience and upbringing has a profound effect on a child's development.

### Mental development early in life

The concepts of 'attachment'[12] and 'resilience'[13] currently inform our attempts to care for children, young people and the socially excluded. To make effective interventions, social workers need to understand the building blocks and nuances of early parental relationships that help children to become resilient through secure attachments with parental figures.

An infant is born totally dependent on his mother or mother substitute. Even before birth, the mother has influenced the development of her baby through her lifestyle and moods, including the use of alcohol and drugs. If she is fearful, perhaps in a violent relationship or anxious, this will be sensed by the baby in the womb. At birth the infant is a collection of sensations held together in his or her skin. The baby gradually develops understanding of his or her boundaries, 'me' and 'not me', and of the arrival of life-sustaining food and love from the mother. But in the first days and weeks, the infant can brook no delay between catastrophic hunger and this being assuaged.

> ## So often a friendly tip can sort out a potential problem
>
> I remember sitting up in bed in a long Nightingale Ward, tearful and anxious with a three-day-old baby bellowing in my arms. A lovely nurse suggested I drew the bed curtains, stripped myself and the baby, and had a bit of 'skin time' to get to know each other. This was perfect advice!

The baby lets the mother feel his persecutory phantasies of 'no food' in his screams of distress. But as the weeks go by the baby begins to grasp that hunger, food and satisfaction are interrelated. Wilfred Bion[14] says that 'an understanding mother is able to experience the feeling of dread that her baby was striving to deal with by projective identification and yet retain a balanced outlook'. A mother needs to be psychologically strong enough to accept the infant's feelings and continue to express her love for the baby when feeding or holding him. The baby takes in and internalises this love as a loving relationship in its psyche, just as he digests milk.

When the distressed baby projects his fear and hate into his mother, she acts as the 'container' of her infant's fears and terror. In her reverie she creates dreamable and, later, thinkable good feelings for the baby to ingest and imagine. Quiet rocking and crooning provide the calming reassurance babies need. These are the outward signs of this process of containment and reflection. The infant will eventually internalise this capacity to manage his feelings and thoughts, and develop his own ability to contain, understand and give them meaning through the use of words.

## What happens if the mother cannot cope?

But sometimes a mother feels her baby's panic and terror as her own. This can immobilise her adult caring capacity. If the mother is unable to act as a receptacle for the baby's projections, he may continue to project feelings of hate to rid himself of the persecutory phantasies from his unmet need for food and love. This can lead to a deadening passivity and the destruction of the infant's impulse to be curious, on which his learning and development depend. It might also lead to hatred of others as the withholders of all good things.

> ## The effects of crack cocaine addiction on the daughters of addicts
>
> Twenty years ago there was an epidemic of crack cocaine use in the local housing estates. Fifteen or so years later, a handful of very young mothers were referred for assessment to the charity, St Michael's Fellowship. They were unable to respond to their babies in an empathetic and reassuring way. They had received no love or emotional care from their addicted mothers, and had failed to build up a store of good feelings inside themselves with which to reassure and love their own babies.
>
> The mothers could not put their babies' needs before their own needs. They experienced the baby's cries as an accusation of inadequacy which made them feel terrible. They had expected their babies to give them the unconditional love their mothers had tragically failed to provide.

Occasionally another nurturing adult can step into the gap left by the neglectful mother – an auntie or nana – and provide the young child with the needed affection. But without that opportunity, the child is likely to need an alternative carer. Social workers are faced with the challenge of supporting service users from this background and confronting the truth when a mum cannot put her baby's needs first. There is a need to help such women find a way forward to live a sustainable life in the community without their children who have new carers.

## A facilitating environment to allow positive feeling when away from mother

Donald Winnicott[15] identified 'potential' or 'transitional' space between the infant and the mother as space of creativity and play. He and Clare Winnicott also explored transitional objects from their work with young evacuees.[16] He considered the way that babies acquire 'transitional objects', that not-me but yet very close object, for example a piece of muslin, a teddy or a blanket. He noted how these can act as a symbol for a mother's actual presence at the boundaries of sleeping and waking, of being together and separating. He believed the baby invests the object with meaning and content, which enables it to stand in for the mother in other situations. This allows transitional objects to be an emotional lifeline to many small children, giving them the sense of security needed to manage new strange situations.

---

### My granddaughter's transitional object

At the end of the day my three-year-old granddaughter wanted her 'Duckie' to join in her game of Lego. Reluctant to climb two flights of stairs, I offered her another teddy. 'Oh that's just a toy – I need Duckie', she said, making it clear that the latter was far more than a toy.

---

The facilitating environment can contain and hold the baby in the mother's absence. The infant can manage to be alone and separate, if there is the sense that 'the mother is reliably present, even if represented for the moment by a cot, pram or the general atmosphere of the immediate environment'.[17] This can take place at an early stage, with the amount of ego support needed from the mother gradually reducing. Eventually the infant is able to tolerate the actual absence of the mother. Flash-backs can occur in adulthood when there is a particular positive feel about a place or situation. Proust had madeleines dipped in tea – I find shadows of leaves on a wall take me straight back to rest time as a toddler.

### Acceptance of the relationship between parents

Ron Britton[18] suggested that, while the main focus of this stage in the child's development is the relinquishing of an exclusive relationship with one parent and the mourning of that loss, the child's acceptance of the parents' joint relationship provides another perspective. By accepting it, the child is now part of a triangular relationship. This gives him the potential to be 'a participant in a relationship observed by a third person, and being an observer of a relationship between two people'. Many parents have seen their children resist acceptance of the second parent – 'Let Daddy speak!' is a common plea – but by the age of four, children are confident in both parents' love and can let them talk together uninterrupted.

The triangular space formed by these benign relationships serves as a space outside the self, called 'the third position'. This is then 'capable of being observed and thought about'. In this third position, the child can not only observe the relationship between his parents but appreciate that he too can be observed. This lets us 'entertain another point of view while retaining our own, to reflect on ourselves while being ourselves'.

Peter Fonagy describes the ability to form representations of other people's thoughts without direct experience oneself as 'the capacity to conceive of conscious and unconscious mental states in oneself and others'.[19] He thought this mental development, linked with the development of concern and empathy, probably starts in a child at the end of its first year and becomes fully active at the age of three or four. It is always so touching when young children start to express concern for their care-giver – for example, sharing food, making sure they are warm, etc.

Someone who has no empathy or concern for other people at all is usually considered to have psychopathic tendencies, and could be a potential risk to the community. Such an individual may have had an emotionally impoverished infancy, and reacted by withdrawing from any emotional relationship.

---

### Mrs O'Sullivan's son with psychopathic behaviour

The O'Sullivan family dominated my time throughout one summer. Having fathered three sons, dad kept his distance in a local hostel while mum tried to keep her two extrovert teenage boys on the right side of the law.

On one occasion, she tipped off the police station that a 'hot' TV was on the pavement by the telephone box, and complained to me when they failed to collect it! Mrs O'Sullivan believed in the confidentiality of the social work relationship, knowing that I would not tell the police. By the following year, the two older boys had calmed down and moved to more law-abiding hobbies.

Later the youngest boy, slightly built like his dad and receiving little affection from his mother, demonstrated psychopathic behaviour. He was expelled from secondary school for threatening a neighbour with a dinner knife. Ten years later, when I read in the local newspaper that he had committed a murder in adulthood, I remembered the lack of affection in his childhood due to an absent father and a mother lavishing attention on the other siblings.

---

Both of these examples (above and below) illustrate how children with seemingly similar upbringings can have very different emotional experiences within the family or the care environment. Parents are, of course, well aware of the remarkable innate differences between their children.

## William and Joe – one with and one without internalised good feelings

In some cases the social worker is forced to acknowledge that there is little that can be done for some service users with difficult personality disorders. I moved William, aged three, to join his brother Joe in a small group home. But Joe, aged seven, lacking internalised good feelings and had already built a defensive carapace to block out the world. He needed specialist help and moved to a home for troubled boys, where he was a bit of a loner. In his late teens Joe hit a youth outside a pub who was found dead after Joe had fled, leading to a tough prison sentence. Social work care had been unable to reach him.

In contrast, though William's housemother died suddenly on the job when he was four years old, he had the inner resources to soldier on – thanks largely to the loving care of a foster mother in the first 16 months of his life. The boys' mother died through an accidental overdose of drugs on release from prison when he was aged five and Joe was eight. I remember that I could not stop crying during a session at the local child guidance clinic. I was comforted by the clinician's phrase, 'It's OK – someone needs to mourn this young woman.'

William grew up and found a job and a steady girlfriend. He was on course aged 20 to live a satisfactory life in the community. The affectionate care of a foster mother from birth to 16 months and social work support, based on emotional warmth and empowerment, had been successful.

## Organisational containment

Wilfred Bion expanded his concept of the maternal role of containment to suggest that institutions, such as a social services department, provide a containing function for their members. Anyone who has exchanged office life alongside a group of colleagues for solitary home working (as I did on moving to Topss England) will be well aware of the usually supportive nature of the organisational setting and miss this support if based away from an office. But the dysfunctional and unhelpful relationships that can sometimes occur between different subgroups in organisations also need to be recognised.[20]

Just as the baby projects his intolerable anxieties and fears onto his mother, institutions, which deal with the difficult emotions brought by distressed people, have to manage their defences against the anxiety, hostility and guilt both within the organisation and externally in society. Social workers can be affected both as professionals and as individuals. Groups survive by splitting off their ambivalent and hostile feelings and projecting them onto colleagues in other groups.

Anton Obholzer points out that organisations such as the social or health services 'deal constantly with fundamental human anxieties about life, death and annihilation'.[21] 'The individual who is prey to these primitive anxieties seeks relief by projecting them into another.' The process of containment allows these feelings to become bearable. Similarly, the social services 'serve to contain these anxieties for society as a whole'. Underlying tensions due to challenging clients cannot be managed 'by denying and repressing them as that invariably leads to further difficulties and disturbance'. This may need professional understanding of the group involvement in projection, splitting and counter-transference. Managers can benefit from expert assistance in confronting these forces to ensure that particular groups are not unfairly scapegoated in the organisation.

## Marginalisation of seriously dependent people

Social workers are often ambivalent about service users becoming dependent on them. Is it allowed? Will they be trapped into spending more time than expected? Will they be overwhelmed by this person's needs, and taken over by the situation? But there is a risk for severely dependent people of being objectified and then depersonalised. This gives rise to the danger of abuse by their carers.

Donald Winnicott suggests that psychiatric practice could benefit if psychiatrists and mental health staff were in touch with the hate and fear of their psychotic patients that were projected into them. 'However much he loves his patients he cannot avoid hating them and fearing them, and the better he knows this the less will hate and fear be the motives determining what he does to his patients.'[22] This needs to be borne in mind by staff in mental health services, services for people with physical and learning disabilities, and services for older people.

## The need to reduce the risk of abuse by carers

There is a risk that service users such as Mr J, whom the nursing home wanted to move, are treated with lack of individuality and respect. In extreme cases this can lead to seriously inappropriate treatment or possibly abuse, as happened at the Mid-Staffordshire NHS Foundation Trust.[23]

Hospital social workers are in the front line to protect vulnerable and dependent people. But total institutions can have difficulty in hearing the warning bells of 'the potential sadistic abuse of the power that staff have over patients'.[24] Bells rang for me in a case discussion at a team meeting when a resident was said to have been denied appropriate help with toileting, and again when the operations manager described the efficiency of his IT spreadsheets for moving patients mechanistically through the system to provide the empty beds needed by the hospital.

---

### Matthew – handling an allegation of abuse

Occasionally a social worker has to consider carefully allegations of abuse and make a difficult judgement call.

I had a day-time emergency call to jump on a train to visit a small private boys' boarding school in the West Country and interview a 14-year-old from my local authority. Another boy from our local authority had complained of a young master putting his arm round him. Matthew, my charge, had little time for the allegation, saying that the master was one of the kinder members of staff. As the master had now been suspended and the boy was willing to stay till the end of term, we agreed he should discuss future plans for his education with a permanent social worker, when appointed.

---

## Helping with decision making

Is there any way that routine social work interventions could reduce the risk for vulnerable adults? From my observation in the hospital, a first step would be to engage with service users and discuss planned placements – encouraging them to share their doubts and fears, rather than succumb to the conveyor belt of care. Those with the faculties to appreciate their predicament would be enabled to reach some understanding of the drastic moves which they were being required to make.

A further step would be to obtain details of a patient's past life and contacts so these can be handed on to a new residence as a start of a 'life story book'. A friend prepared such a book of photographs for her mother, who was then able to interest her East European carers in her earlier years as a missionary's wife around the world.

---

### Emily – coming to terms with an unwelcome move

Emily moved in her late eighties into a purpose-built ground-floor flat close to her friends and neighbours. Five years later, she had a couple of nasty falls and wanted to find a nearby residential home. Her only relative was a nephew in her home town 120 miles away. The cost of local residential care was beyond her means, and her nephew thought that she should join her sister-in-law in a home near him.

Emily hated the idea and the conflict on what to do upset her. She became short tempered and anxious. She had left home aged 20 in 1940 to work in the church during the war, and had built her life around that. We talked together, lamenting the losses from a move, but I reminded her of the guts that she had shown when younger and that she still had the ability to make the move in a way that would work out.

This helped Emily to remember her internal strengths and put her in the right frame of mind to make the decision to join her sister-in-law. She accepted help from younger friends in packing up – and then settled in quickly and was content with the change.

---

### Comment

People who have not had a loving and containing adult to nurture them when very young are likely to lack internalised good feelings about themselves and others. They take a substantial proportion of the efforts of social workers. William and Joe illustrate the huge difference in the direction in life path of two siblings. One developed psychopathic behaviour, while the other has been able to live a satisfactory life, benefiting from an affectionate foster mother and social work support.

### Notes

1 Younghusband, E. 1974. 'Foreword'. In: F. Turner (ed.), *Social work treatment: interlocking theoretical approaches*. New York: Free Press, p. 24.
2 Winnicott, D. 1965. 'The mentally ill on your caseload'. In: Winnicott, D. *The maturational processes and the facilitating environment*. London: Karnac.

3 Moriarty, J. and Manthorpe, J. March 2016. 'The effectiveness of social work with adults'. Social Care Workforce Research Unit, King's College London.

4 Miller, E.J. and Gwynne, G.V. 1972. *A life apart: a pilot study of residential institutions for the physically handicapped and the young chronic sick*. London: Tavistock.

5 *The Guardian*. 21 March 2016. 'Operation Midland: how the Met lost its way'.

6 Cooper, A. 2005. 'Surface and depth in the Victoria Climbié Inquiry Report'. *Child and Family Social Work* 10: 1–9.

7 American Psychiatric Association. 1987. *Diagnostic and statistical manual for mental disorders*. 3rd edn. Washington, DC: American Psychiatric Press.

8 Garland, C. 1991. 'External disasters and the internal world: an approach to psychotherapeutic understanding of survivors'. In: J. Holmes (ed.). *Textbook of psychotherapy in psychiatric practice*. London: Churchill Livingstone Longmans.

9 Hoggett, P. 2000. *Emotional life and the politics of welfare*. London: Macmillan.

10 Government response to Winterbourne View. December 2012.

11 *The Mirror*. 29 October 2013. 'Disabled man burnt to death by vigilantes who wrongly suspected him of being a paedophile'.

12 Ainsworth, M. 1977. 'Social development in the first year of life: maternal influences on infant-mother attachment'. In: J. Tanner (ed.), *Developments in psychiatric research*. London: Hodder & Stoughton; Bowlby, J. 1979. *The making and breaking of affectional bonds*. London: Tavistock.

13 Reivich, K. and Shatte, A. 2002. *The resilience factor*. New York: Broadway Books.

14 Bion, W. 1962. *Learning from experience*. London: Karnac.

15 Winnicott, D. 1971. *Playing and reality*. Harmondsworth: Penguin.

16 Kantor, J. 2004. *Face to face with children*. London: Karnac.

17 Winnicott, D. 1965. 'The capacity to be alone'. In: Winnicott, D. *The maturational processes and the facilitating environment*. London: Karnac.

18 Britton, R. 1989. 'The missing link: parental sexuality in the Oedipus complex'. In: Britton, R., Feldman, M. and O'Shaughnessy, E. *The Oedipus complex today: clinical implications*. London: Karnac.

19 Fonagy, P. 1991. 'Thinking about thinking: some clinical and theoretical considerations in the treatment of a borderline patient'. *International Journal of Psychoanalysis* 72: 639–665.

20 Menzies, I. 1970. *The functioning of social systems as a defence against anxiety*. London: Tavistock Institute of Human Relations.

21 Obholzer, A. and Roberts, V.Z. (eds). 1994. *The unconscious at work*. London: Routledge, pp. 169–170.

22 Winnicott, D. 1947. 'Hate in the counter-transference'. *International Journal of Psychoanalysis* 30: 69–75.

23 The Francis Report (Report of the Mid-Staffordshire NHS Foundation Trust public inquiry) 2013.

24 Dartington, A. 1994. 'Where angels fear to tread: idealism, despondency and inhibition of thought in hospital nursing'. In: A. Obholzer and V.Z. Roberts (eds), *The unconscious at work*. London: Routledge.

# 3

# ENGAGING WITH SERVICE USERS

This chapter describes how social workers relate to and engage with service users. This is an essential professional skill and the first vital step allowing reflection on the emotional issues of a service user. The chapter then sets out how social workers use their ability to reflect creatively and professional judgement to decide on an appropriate intervention.

Georgio's story indicates his emotional instability and constant need for reassurance, and how he had found a temporary way to manage his anxieties.

---

**Talking a service user out of drowning himself**

My intake team had daily conversations with Georgio, who called in to the office for a cup of tea and cigarette or rang from a telephone box by the river, threatening to jump in until diverted by a reassuring talk.

'I feel like jumping, I've had enough.'

'Oh, Georgio, don't do that. How about a ciggie and then come up to us for a cuppa?'

'Oh, all right, just one.'

---

Liz's story indicates that relating to a service user is not always straightforward.

---

**Liz's story – a service user who is difficult to engage**

Liz, a very competent experienced locum worker in the District Team told me about the problem she was facing with one service user. This story shows she was trying to decide a way forward through case discussion with other agencies, but finding the service user challenging:

'Thinking of difficult cases, I have one chappy who's in his early 50s. He's HIV positive and says it's a secret even from his family. He's very cautious about who knows – he didn't want us to know – so we're working with someone who is a very private person. But his needs are quite great because he's very lame with arthritis and can't do very much for himself at all. So he needs personal and domestic care.

*(continued)*

31

*(continued)*

He's a challenge to work with because he's so demanding. Whenever we get him an agency worker nothing is ever right. I understand really because I'd find it difficult having someone coming into my house.

He has been in daily contact with me since February and we are now in June – blaming us and saying it's our fault that the help is not perfect. We did send him away for two weeks on respite care – it wasn't just me but his specialist nurse who was also overwhelmed. Everyone who comes into contact with him has a hard time and you have to pussyfoot around. We're having a meeting tomorrow with two different agencies at his home to sort out a plan. For personal care he wants a white English male, and then for his domestic work he has accepted an offer of a black woman who is very good. But where does personal care end and domestic support start? We just have to iron out the little bits.

He wants the flexibility to ask the personal care worker to bring in the washing. He doesn't want to hear that it's not in the job description. I can understand that but that's the way the agency work is split. And we all say "Yes it must be flexible and reasonable" – but in reality it depends on the home care workers. Is the care worker going to keep quiet and do a few tasks out of the ordinary?

I can't wait to let go of him, he makes you feel you've done everything wrong! So he's one of the most difficult cases I've ever had – not because of his physical disabilities but because of himself. He's a nice enough guy – so it's difficult to pinpoint what the problem is with him'.

On reflection, the problem for Liz was that the service user was successfully projecting his panic, anger and frustration at his physical pain and disabilities on to her and everyone else trying to shore up his care.

It is inevitably difficult to relate to someone who cannot easily respond. Family members are often able to find their own level of communication by interpreting small signs from an unconscious, brain-damaged or dementing person. People's individuality can engage with us in many ways.

### Troy – speechless but able to stick out his tongue

Physically dependent people can recruit help through their own personalities. Troy, aged six, was abandoned and speechless in hospital with his limbs confined to prevent self-harm from chronic muscle spasms. I was a young nursing auxiliary and taught him to stick his tongue out at the matron. When I visited six months later he greeted me with a wide grin and stuck out his tongue! The ability to relate is vital if service users are to protect and to preserve themselves.

One social worker in the District Team summed this up. 'Younger adults are in tune with what is happening around them. They may be disabled but they are very alert mentally. You have to be very clued up with the information you have as they are constantly challenging what you are talking about.'

## Ways that social workers can engage with borderline service users

It can be particularly challenging to work with non-compliant service users. More social workers need to develop skills to do this. The specific knowledge and skills were shared with colleagues in the probation service until the shared social work education and training was scrapped by the Conservative government in the 1990s. Social workers also need to understand the most appropriate way to contain and help people with common mental health issues, such as anxiety and depression or with borderline personalities. People's needs can cross the bureaucratic support boundaries between health and social care, and it might not be straightforward to decide interventions.

---

### Engaging with a mentally ill and frightened young man with a knife

Sometimes engagement is problematic. I had to ensure the safety of a frightened young man. He had grabbed a knife and run to the top of his family's house. The sister had shouted out 'Call the police' from the window, 'He says he is Jesus Christ'. He was surrounded by helpful friends including a Rastafarian preacher who had arrived by cab. I found he was known to the mental health services. The whole street turned out to watch while a duty doctor and I went in to talk to him.

However we could not wind back the situation because more and more police arrived. They rushed en masse into the house, and pressed the poor man to the floor. We all accompanied him to the nearby accident and emergency department of the local hospital. I told the family that they should just call a doctor next time and not the police. So much upset could have been avoided if colleagues had followed up this distressed person in the days before.

---

## Good enough ways for the social worker to engage positively

In these type of testing situations, the social worker needs to remain clear and firm, unbothered by hysteria or displays of anger or frustration. A study[1] lists 'good enough ways the social worker could engage positively with a borderline service user, who needs the social worker to be a specific figure:

- who will become familiar
- with whom they can form a relationship within which emotional issues can be raised
- who is reliable and trustworthy
- who can survive and acknowledge anger and failure on his part and that of his client
- who is good enough, not totally bad nor trying to be totally good
- who can encourage the client's own efforts
- who can share and cooperate
- who can leave in a way that is not too traumatic.'

---

### Mrs Z: a hard to engage family

The District Team were finding it difficult to engage with Mrs Z who was confined to a wheelchair by a degenerative disease. The housing department had not been able to visit and were worried that she was being neglected. Her husband would not let anyone in. When the social worker had offered an assessment, Mr Z had refused. While the team was considering what to do, he had a massive heart attack. Aged only 38 years old, he was now in hospital with severe brain damage. Their 18-year-old son had left home and could not continue to care for his mother. So the team needed to arrange emergency respite care for her while a long-term plan was made.

Two months later she was enjoying living in a residential care home, though the youngest resident by far. Her parents were also supportive. The social worker told me that the use of Section 47[2] to 'rescue' her would have been heavy-handed – so perhaps it had all worked out for the best.

---

Donald Winnicott provided a similar list for social workers with mentally ill clients and remarked that:

> The more psychotic or insane disorders are formed in relation to failures in environmental provision, and they can be treated, sometimes successfully, by new environmental provision and this may be through your social work relationship when:

- you apply yourself to the case
- you get to know what it feels like to be your client
- you become reliable for the limited field of your professional responsibility
- you behave professionally
- you concern yourself with your client's problem
- you accept love without flinching and without acting-out your response
- you accept hate and meet it with strength rather than with revenge
- you tolerate your client's illogicality, unreliability, suspicion, muddle, fecklessness, meanness etc., and recognise all the unpleasantnesses as symptoms of distress
- you are not frightened, nor do you become overcome with guilt-feelings when your client goes mad, disintegrates, runs out in the street in a nightdress, attempts suicide and perhaps succeeds. If murder threatens you call in the police to help not only yourself but also the client. In all these emergencies you recognise the client's call for help, or a cry of despair because of loss of hope of help.[3]

The Mental Health Team's operating brief seemed to reflect this list closely.

---

### Sashaying to 'Baby Love' during a mental health admission

Emergency duty work certainly requires rapid understanding of a situation and empathetic engagement with the service user. For a mental health admission on a Sunday afternoon, an agitated young woman was reluctant to come and it was essential to gain

---

her trust. I managed to coax her into a car with The Supremes belting out 'Baby Love', while the policeman, my client and I sashayed to the music. When I heard that she had been very agitated the previous week, I did not thank my colleague for leaving her admission to the weekend – despite the good tunes!

## The disturbing power of projections

Social work teams need to contain and continuously decontaminate the projections absorbed from their clients and society. This requires an ability to understand and transform these frightening primitive fears into something that can be thought about in supportive mental space. Without this opportunity to transform and purge the unconscious of negative projections, the social worker's psyche will gradually become choked – potentially leading to illness, burn-out and even breakdown.

### An attack on a social worker

A social worker in the District Team described a frightening incident: 'The client was shouting "evil bastard!" at the top of his voice as he chased me down the corridor. It was such a scary incident – I was running to save my skin!' She had anticipated trouble and asked for a colleague to accompany her. But the manager had been unable to spare anyone from duty. A subsequent failure to debrief – acknowledging the horror of the incident and providing appropriate support – left the social worker physically unwell and acutely depressed.

Understandably, social workers working with such people need reassurance that they are doing a good job and maintaining the necessary professional–client boundary. I remember a psychoanalyst who accepted a young woman into her hostel only on condition that I saw her weekly. I have never felt so useless as after these sessions and needed the analyst's reassurance that these feelings came from my young client.

### Paranoid phantasies when a client was a neighbour

This process of transforming negative projections can be difficult. I had been advised on my social work training not to live 'on the patch' as there could be unanticipated conflicts. But in the 1970s with the integrated development of community work, the first rounds of house price inflation and favourable mortgage terms for council employees, I was discreetly tucked down a local cul de sac. However, it was difficult when a colleague's client and family became neighbours.

Residents complained about all night parties and other incidents. The client and I both held paranoid phantasies about each other. She imagined that I had organised a petition against her, and I suspected that she had deliberately planned her rave the evening before our child's christening. These phantasies eventually ended when she moved to another borough. I feel as uneasy writing this now as I did then.

## Knowing when to stand back and when to intervene

Social workers in the referral and assessment teams need to decide in a timely way whether support is appropriate and from which team. On setting up the intake team, we agreed that referrals should be handled within six weeks or transferred to the longer term teams. The procedure worked well for people with mental health emergencies, who could be allocated after assessment or admission, and for older people who were content to have a regular visitor after an assessment.

But we learnt that families in crisis do not transfer well. The heightened emotions of the crisis made the decisions of the duty social worker of great significance for the client. The client was often totally committed to the person who had intervened, and confident in their skills and power. Hence it made sense for that social worker to continue to work with the client. For example, Johnny, aged 10, refused to cooperate with anyone other than Jane, who had been involved in his reception into care, and would not be reallocated to suit the system!

Despite these time constraints, it is vital that social workers reflect on whether an intervention is likely to be of any value and, if so, when this might be appropriate. Margot Waddell[4] considered the relationship between thinking and doing for social workers. She divided this into servicing ('doing and acting for someone'), and serving ('the capacity to stand by, one's own internal resources at the ready'). In some cases intervention is inappropriate, for example, there was limited support that could be offered to the McGee family, described next, who had their own way of solving problems.

---

### The McGee family – users who create misunderstanding

There are also manipulative service users who are difficult to fathom. The McGee family was an example. They were being made homeless as Mrs McGee's husband had failed to pay the rent. Their children were in their teens. One was at school and the other two in good jobs with prospects. There was a standard procedure for eviction into homeless family temporary accommodation, which was available for the school-age child and parents. The working offspring were staying with friends.

I soon found that Mr McGee simply could not follow or cooperate with any guidance or advice. Everything had to be arranged through a friend or in the pub, where I had to meet him. I asked him to produce three quotations for furniture removal as required by social security.

'Well Mrs Foster, I have this friend, see, and he can do this for me for £10.'

We went round and round in circles.

Mrs McGee was practised in extricating herself and her daughter from this treacle. I was an absolute beginner and left them to it! I heard later that Mrs McGee found an office job and a nice little bedsitter for her and her daughter, while Mr McGee moved in with a pal from the pub.

---

### Mental space to reflect and decide an appropriate intervention

Our ability to think clearly about difficult emotional issues is closely bound up with our ability to maintain a contained space within our minds – where we can keep our thoughts, feelings and experience, and connect them to the past and present. Social workers need to reflect on many aspects of clients. These include their hopes and dreams, their sadness and despair, their anger and deviousness.

Sometimes when we are unable to think clearly because of an overload of impressions or some strong emotion, we find it helpful to distance ourselves from the material by talking through issues with another person. This can be a colleague or supervisor, who acts as an independent container and reinforces our mental space. Often this is enough to help us to feel 'grounded' and connected back to our internalised memories of good relationships, and hence able to see a way through a situation.

We can ponder what we could offer to make a difference. It is not always what we imagine. One carer told me in the margins of a committee meeting, 'I don't want the social worker to *do* anything – I just want her to come and hear what it is like for me looking after Sally', clearly stating her need to have the social worker 'hold' her feelings about caring for her handicapped child.

I should have reflected more on my relationship with Barry (described next), and my significance as his social worker for his emotional well-being.

---

### Barry – the need to recognise deep attachment to the social worker

Usually I had a clear understanding of the significance of my relationship with children who were in care. But I was brought up short by Barry's reaction. He had been living in a small group home for most of his childhood, and was now aged 11. The staff in the home were important to him, and he valued his relationship with the former children's officer (the 'queen bee' of the old children's department).

Though I had been his social worker over three years, I had never felt particularly important to him. However, when I told him over lunch one day that I was moving on, he said of course he knew that. Staff in the home had told him weeks ago. He was shocked that I had told him with so little notice. I had totally underestimated the significance of our relationship.

Whenever I hear social workers – or usually ex-social workers – referring to their 'cases', I wonder how the actual families and individuals regard them.

---

I learnt from some of my mistakes and did a better job in reflecting on how to help a young girl about to go through a major transition in her life.

---

### June – supporting an important transition in a child's life

Problems of geographical separation are common. Social workers have to handle placements with great sensitivity. The nurseries of inner city conurbations are often by the seaside. Visits required demanding excursions. Specialist boarding schools presented similar access difficulties.

June aged four was separated from her brother and sister at such a nursery. When she was nearly six years old she had an assessment for special educational needs. The

*(continued)*

*(continued)*

psychologist and I agreed that, despite her limited language skills, she would benefit from education at a boarding school in the neighbouring county.

Remembering my experience of childhood moves and June's need for concrete experience, I arranged an overnight visit for her to see the school, before going there permanently the following week. This gave her nursery workers and me an opportunity to talk about the move, and help her to understand what was happening. The school were so impressed by the way June settled in that they introduced this as a routine procedure.

### *Mental space for social workers through reflective supervision*

Social work teams have the challenging task of working in emotionally painful environments, while needing to think creatively and objectively about the emotional and material needs of service users. Social work best practice assumes that regular supervision sessions are held between the social worker and manager, where issues are discussed and resolved. Traditionally, the three ingredients of casework supervision were monitoring social workers' cases; supporting, containing and listening; and advising and discussing techniques and concepts. The provision of supervision has been a key development tool for social workers, but surveys over the decades have always found it wanting.

In recent years the renaissance of relationship-based social work[5] has stressed the need for reflective supervision – with a focus on the interaction of the feelings held by the client and by the social worker. This enhances understanding of the emotions and relationships that underlie the dynamics of the case. Mental space includes all the opportunities for thinking during the working day. Robert Fleming noted:

> To properly finance a department of professionals to work with the crises of human lives, one needs to budget strategically for space to allow the professional to think clearly about the complex situations facing them. To avoid this is not to understand the true costs involved.[6]

Each day every social worker has a problem – how much time can they spend thinking and planning what to do on a case, and how much should they spend in pre-arranged meetings about other service users on their case load? Meetings can easily squeeze out the necessary individual thinking time.

### The value of supervision in my intake team

- Supervision was important in my intake team. The social workers were in our late twenties and thirties, with the exception of our child minding specialist who was in her fifties with offspring aged from 16 to 26. I was touched when she shared a family worry that was impinging on her work. She was worried as her husband had just lost his job in a vicious management carve-up. She trusted the confidentiality of our supervision, and that this upsetting family pressure would be contained within the session.

- On another occasion a young Australian social worker alone in the UK had needed support over a cancer scare that was fortunately negative. She later valued the insight in our supervision that her reluctance to visit a patient her own age with cancer may have been linked to this trauma. She then found the confidence to contact and help the young woman.

## The reduction in use of supervision

The General Social Care Council achieved much in its short life by introducing individual registration of social workers in 2004 and an underpinning post-qualifying framework. Social workers became responsible for updating their own professional skills as in the nursing and medical field. This needs a culture in which supervision and other structures are part of a learning[7] and reflective environment.[8]

The Social Care Institute for Excellence identified eight key learning settings in organisations:

1 supervision
2 team meetings
3 post-qualifying or advanced award mentoring
4 practice teaching
5 in-service training
6 individual continuous professional development
7 service user and carer participation
8 other meetings such as briefings for local authority councillors.

This list omits working in pairs, which was demonstrably successfully as a learning method in the Mental Health Team. Perhaps this omission reflects social work's limited resources and conservative approach to working practices. From the 1980s the counselling/case work role in social work received less emphasis and thereby there was less demand for managers to develop reflective supervision skills.[9]

### Content of supervision

The next story explores the process of thinking through the content of an interview.

## Jill's tale of a dying mother and how she ruminated on the situation

Jill, a social worker in the District Team, was asked to assess a young mother for home care services. The client was dying of a brain tumour and Jill found herself in the centre of a tragic denouement. The following shows the development of Jill's thinking as she ruminated on her observations from the third position.

'I am working with a lady in her thirties. Her position is very sad. And most worrying for her is her relationship. She is a Scottish lady married to a Muslim; they

*(continued)*

39

*(continued)*

have two young children. She's very isolated from her family because of the drama associated with her marriage. She has a brain tumour and epilepsy and she is very poorly. She was difficult to get in touch with. When I visited her at home, I came across her husband. I was astonished – I have never known anyone to be so horrid. He gave her the divorce papers as I sat on the bed. I thought "She is dying." I was there when this happened.

I was dumbfounded. I don't doubt the fact that he is absolutely fed up with her. But he said "She has medication – she doesn't have to be sick." I said, "I'm going to have to stop you. I don't think you really understand what is happening." He said "What do you mean?" A little smile came on her face. She honestly thought somebody was at last sticking up for her. I thought "This poor woman has to put up with this man. How on earth must she feel about these things?"

Bless her, she went into hospital the next day. I phoned yesterday and spoke to her and then to him because he cares for the children. He adores his children and they are his world. In his way he does cares for her indirectly. He has to tidy the home and he will cook a meal, so she could benefit that way. She lives with their children and he lived separately.

Then I thought "This hasn't suddenly happened, he must have been like this in the past. She thought she could live with it but now she realises that she's stuck." It is very sad. When I said goodbye to her, she said she just wanted somebody to talk to. As the children came at the weekend, he's not bringing them back until the end of the week.

So there she is all poorly and with no children and no one else. So I said "I tell you what. If they leave a little window in my day, I will come to see you." She said "Okay, thank you." So that's where we left it.' Jill paused, then continued with renewed vigour: 'So I *will* put it down that I'm doing a visit. *That's* what I'll do.'

This story shows the development of Jill's resolution to visit the dying young mother. She used our interview to understand and reflect on what was really happening in the family. This gave Jill the opportunity to rethink the role of the father from 'being so horrid' to 'by cooking, tidying and caring for the children he cares for her indirectly'. She then realised that her client had a part in how things had turned out: 'This hasn't suddenly happened.'

Jill had made a deep connection with the young mother during that first traumatic confrontation. Through reflection, the social worker was able to make a realistic plan – that the dying mother might find it helpful to talk to her. Jill no longer expected to make the marriage different, but wanted to give the mother some supportive space at the end of her life.

The lack of regular supervision has been a constant complaint over the last 30 years. Even when supervision happens, it can often feel inspectorial. Lord Laming recommended that 'Directors of Social Services must ensure that the work of staff working directly with children is regularly supervised. This must include the supervisor reading, reviewing, and signing the case file at regular intervals'.[10] Twenty years earlier, Mary

Barker, my supervisor on Brunel University's master's programme, offered an alternative view on a similar tragedy:

> The social worker needs supportive supervision if she is to face the realities of some of her most distressed and disturbed clients, because defensive denial of some of the emotional and social realities inevitably means that the information available for thinking, judging and acting is impoverished and quite possibly faulty as a result.[11]

---

### Ian – reflecting about a boy from a secure unit during emergency duty

Ian was an experienced member of an emergency duty team and former colleague, who was willing to be interviewed following a duty session. Prompted by his notes, he talked about each of the cases that had arisen. I noticed that after each case he said 'So that one went away!' alerting me that his view of the primary task was to despatch referrals elsewhere.

The final case was a messy situation about a teenage boy from a secure unit in the care of his father. He was barred from visiting his mother and siblings. An agency worker had been engaged to check up on the boy during working hours. This had apparently involved the police and further raised the profile of the case. Ian had come across the situation three days before, when he was duty officer. But he had been given no information on relevant telephone numbers or emergency accommodation arrangements – let alone any wider plans for the boy. That evening the boy had his father's permission to be out from 6.30 to 11.30 pm and *did* go round to his mother's house.

Ian managed to speak to her: 'She told me they had a huge argument and he smashed up the younger brother's computer but he's now left. So I thought "Well?" Then I got a terrible headache myself. It's terribly unusual for me to be off sick, but another Mental Health Act assessment came in at 10.30 and I managed to get somebody else to cover for me for three hours.'

Ian described how he could not face passing on the boy's case to the second worker but slept for three hours, officially going back on duty at 1.30 am. He then became increasingly uneasy as to whether or not the boy had returned to his father. A telephone call in the morning confirmed that he had returned.

The social worker described the general anxiety around the boy and his family, the way the violence of the row had immediately got into his head, temporarily but totally disabling him, and the repercussions for him if anything had gone wrong. As he spoke, he spontaneously thought of a way through the situation. 'I should have rung the father back at 11.30 to see if the child was back. That's what I should have done!' His sudden debilitating headache had deprived him of the ability to think, which the mental space of the interview restored.

By having the space to put his anxieties into words, the projected negative feelings from the case were transformed into thinkable material and allowed constructive thought.

## Mental space for organisations

Inevitably organisations working with people in difficulty have to manage their projections; otherwise they run the risk of replicating the damaged or malfunctioning psyches encountered by staff. The extent to which the organisation manages these processes, creatively or defensively, impacts on the social workers and their work. A considerable body of knowledge relating to the unconscious in organisations has developed since Freud's research.[12]

Each of the three teams that I studied had developed its own distinctive behaviour that seemed to reflect the clients' dilemmas. It was only by being on the outside looking in on the District Team that I had the time to ruminate on the siting of this team at the furthest boundary of the borough. It was totally inaccessible to anyone with a chronic condition and – the final irony – next door to the cemetery. No wonder I concluded that society wanted to bury them all.

### *Changing the organisational culture to a more reflective style*

David Lawlor has analysed the provision of social work supervision from the viewpoint of the organisations' dynamics along with the supervisors' individual skills. He found that 'listening and observing is a skill that supervisors need to acquire. They often feel they have to offer solutions (as their social workers feel with their service users). The rush to action often prevented a fuller and deeper understanding of either the case or the professional difficulties that the worker might be carrying'.[13]

In addition to providing a containing space as in Jill's tale (page 39) and Ian's story (page 41), he recommends enabling questions to prompt the social worker:

- Facilitation: 'I wonder what you mean when you say you are worried about the care of the children?'
- Eliciting: 'Tell me more about the condition of the children.'
- Probing: 'You seem bothered and upset about the way the mother spoke to the children. What exactly bothers you? Why?'
- Observing: 'For the first part of the supervision session I have noticed that you keep going back to concerns about the mother but haven't mentioned the father.'
- Confronting: 'This family seems to be worrying you a great deal. But you seem reluctant to put your cards on the table with the parents on the care of the children.'

Through coaching, social workers can be helped to manage the jumbled impressions, facts and feelings resulting from a meeting. It is from this 'crooked timber of humanity'[14] that they are expected to deduce a course of action to protect the vulnerable and enable carers to improve their care.

### *The need for good systems for social workers to learn from each other*

Lisa Bostock[15] asked three children and families teams about their forums for discussion, reflection and reporting systems to share practice. They found that there were rarely systems in place to learn from each other and no time set aside. Thus any learning came from informal discussions with other team members. A service manager said what was needed was 'not more guidance, procedures, or memos saying "Why aren't you doing things?" but actually some time for reflection, and to chew things over'.

Social workers are best serviced in their place of work if they find:

- emotional containment through colleagues, managers or consultants,
- organisational containment through a competent manager,
- intellectual containment through the culture of the team supporting the integration of knowledge into practice.[16]

---

### Learning from the duty officer how to handle a problem family

My experience of emergency cover for the social services department at evenings and weekends underlined the need to be able to obtain quick advice from colleagues. These were often awkward times when few colleagues were available. An experienced duty officer on the telephones made a big difference. He rang at 11.30 pm one night and said 'It's the Baileys – they had a fight and the dad's left, but he took a knife with him.'

I did not know what I could do to help but recognised a notorious family name and asked 'What should I do?' He replied dolefully, 'We usually visit'. We discussed possible ways forward and I went round. I found Mrs Bailey and two adolescent girls at home, still alarmed by the row. Playing for time, I suggested a cup of tea and asked them to tell me all about it. The concern was 'What would happen when dad came back?' About an hour later he did.

We were all rather scared as he opened the door – but there stood a very short man, much smaller than the three women, who immediately spoke to me in an ingratiating manner. His knife could not be seen, and the women seemed unconcerned. After 20 minutes or so, I suggested that as it was 1.30 am everyone quietly went to bed, which we did!

---

### Turning a blind eye to tragic situations

Margaret Rustin[17] notes how both social workers and the organisation involved in the Victoria Climbié Inquiry appeared to want to escape from thinking about Victoria and her aunt, Kouao. In fact, Kouao's borderline psychotic thinking invaded the social workers' thinking, which became as confused and irrational as Kouao's. Here the concept of 'turning a blind eye' is relevant to defend against overwhelming feelings – the psychic defence of seeing but not seeing such pain and destruction.

It is not only those professionally involved in a dreadful situation who find it hard to face up to the evidence in front of their eyes.[18] While the inquiry was taking place, another child was murdered. This was not in a deprived inner city but in a rural village. The young girl lived with her father and stepmother, next door to her paternal grandparents.[19] People had worries about the situation but no one acted. Over four years her nearest adult relatives and neighbours became accustomed to the sadistic brutality of her stepmother. They turned a blind eye for their own psychological safety. The local Member of Parliament, Gillian Shephard, said the case seemed even worse than Victoria Climbié's 'because it all took place in full view of those people who should have been caring for Lauren'.

It is a relief that we have a built-in emergency emotional brake to survive horrific situations. A social worker fainted giving evidence at a murder trial that involved a youth accused of casually killing a young professional man. She had been his social worker since his flight from his homeland in adolescence. The conflict of emotions can be more than the individual can bear.

John Schneider noted: 'Not knowing is a means of safeguarding one's very existence.'[20] He referred to Freud's suggestion that the evasion of reality is essential for maintaining one's capacity to use one's mind to process incoming stimuli[21] and goes on to say: 'Not perceiving is not simply a failure to perceive; it constitutes a psychic function in its own right: it safeguards our sanity from breakdown as a result of being flooded by more external reality than we can psychologically process.' This indicates why in the Baby P case in 2007, the police, social services and health service – both community and hospital – *all* failed to grasp the risk to the toddler.

## The need for management support on critical cases

Good management and supervision structures are needed to support social workers dealing with these tragic cases. However, Margaret Rustin pointed out how far the working environment in the Victoria Climbié case was from any necessary sharing for the staff:

> Not talking about and not writing down disturbing observations are examples of the avoidance of thought. It was rare in this case that two minds got together to think about what was going on. The people involved seem to have had pitifully few moments of sharing their thoughts.

These stressful cases inevitably have a knock-on effect on the way that social workers work with other service users. They will inevitably bring their experience of such trauma and the anxieties which these have provoked to any new situation. If they receive no support from their managers or office colleagues, the situation will quickly become intolerable.

---

### Feeling fear when alone with a father oiling his shotgun

Before the recognition of high-risk moments in child protection work, I remember my fear when I discussed a child's failed school attendance and possible removal from home. I realised that I was alone in the house with father and son, while the father deliberately cleaned his shotgun in front of me. It was hard to think straight at the time, but the next day I rang the police to explain the situation and was relieved when his gun licence was revoked.

---

The Climbié report uncovered an apparent indifference in the local authority to the standard of services and to the operational well-being of their staff. The anger of the public toward social workers after such tragedies is particularly concerning. In contrast, psychiatrists whose patients kill their babies on ill-advised home leave seem to avoid most of these projections and public blame.

## Comment

Service users can be difficult and awkward and resist forming a relationship. Social workers need a natural aptitude as well as professional training to handle suspicion and unpleasant behaviour. They also need to be able to decontaminate the projections from clients. Supervision and reflective space are an essential part of this, otherwise there is a risk of exhaustion and burn-out. Regrettably the pressures of modern office life have reduced the time for supervision, and there is a need to build a more reflective organisational culture – particularly to prevent a blind eye being turned to tragic and emotionally overwhelming situations.

## Notes

1 Mattinson, J. and Sinclair, I. 1979. *Mate and stalemate*. London: Institute of Marital Studies.
2 National Assistance Act 1948: Section 47 Removal to suitable premises of persons in need of care and attention.
3 Winnicott, D. 1965. 'The mentally ill on your caseload'. In: Winnicott, D. *The maturational processes and the facilitating environment*. London: Karnac.
4 Waddell, M. 1989. *Living in two worlds: psychodynamic theory and social work practice*. Free Associations.
5 Ruch, G., Turney, D. and Ward, A. 2010. *Relationship-based social work: getting to the heart of practice*. London: Jessica Kingsley.
6 Fleming, R. 1998. 'The inner impact of work with disturbance'. In: R. Davies (ed.), *Stress in social work*. London: Jessica Kingsley.
7 Rosen, G., Bairstow, S. and Marsh, P. 2003. Learning Organisations: Project Report. Available from the Social Care Institute for Excellence. London.
8 Ruch, G. 2007. 'Reflective practice in contemporary child-care social work: the role of containment'. *British Journal of Social Work* 37: 659–680.
9 Mattinson, J. 1992. *The reflective process in casework supervision*. 2nd edn. London: Tavistock Institute.
10 Department of Health and Home Office. January 2003. 'Report by Lord Laming on the Victoria Climbié Inquiry'. CM5730. London: The Stationery Office.
11 Barker, M. 1982. 'Through experience towards theory: a psychodynamic contribution to social work education'. *Issues in Social Work Education* 2(1): 3–25.
12 Freud, S. 1922. *Group psychology and the analysis of the ego*. London: Hogarth Press and Institute of Psycho-analysis.
13 Lawlor, D. 2013. 'A transformation programme for children's social care managers'. *Journal of Social Work Practice* 27(2): 177–189.
14 Kant, 1784.
15 Bostock, L., Bairstow, S., Fish, S. and Macleod, F. 2004. *Managing risk within child welfare: promoting safety management and reflective decision-making*. London: Social Care Institute for Excellence.
16 Ruch, G. 2007. 'Reflective practice in contemporary child-care social work'.
17 Rustin, M. 2005. 'Conceptual analysis of critical moments in Victoria Climbié's life'. *Child and Family Social Work* 10: 11–19.

18 Steiner, J. 1985. 'Turning a blind eye: the cover up for Oedipus'. *International Review of Psychoanalysis* 12: 161–172.
19 Lauren Wright. BBC News 1 October 2001. http://news.bbc.co.uk/1/hi/england/1573 910.stm
20 Schneider, J.A. 2005. 'Experiences in K and –K'. *International Journal of Psychoanalysis* 86: 825–839.
21 Freud, S. 1920. 'Beyond the pleasure principle'. In: *The standard edition of the complete psychological works of Sigmund Freud. Vol. XVIII.* London: Hogarth Press, 1955, pp. 3–64.

# 4

# BENEATH THE SURFACE OF THREE TEAMS

This chapter covers my study of day-to-day practice in three different social work teams to identify the necessary supporting factors for effective practice. The three social work teams were comparable in size and geography, all working with adults, but in differing circumstances. There was a District Team for younger adults (aged 19–64); a Hospital Team under pressure to facilitate discharges in the same borough; and a Mental Health Team in a different borough. The principal officer, Dawn, managed the first two teams. The specialist Mental Health Team worked with the homeless mentally ill. The field work was completed in 12 months, with a total of 44 visits and 37 interviews across the three teams.

At the time of my research, one borough was restructuring its services and removing two layers of management. When I negotiated the contract, there was: a director of adult services, an assistant director, and a principal officer who managed three teams delivering adult services. I was with the 'younger adults' service manager (of the District Team) and the hospital service manager (of the Hospital Team) who both had three team leaders. The Mental Health Team for homeless mentally ill people was part of a Mental Health Trust that covered two local authority boroughs. The part-time social work manager reported to a senior social work manager in the trust.

## THE DISTRICT SOCIAL WORK TEAM

The District Team carried out assessments and arranged care services for adults aged 19–64 with chronic debilitating illnesses. The team invited me to meet their manager, Andy. The team of 21 people was based at the far end of the borough in a large first-floor open-plan office. Six officers from another department sat at one bank of desks in the room. There was a shared reception on the ground floor and interviewing rooms tucked round the corner. (See Appendix 2 page 133) for an extract from my record of a day at the District Team.)

### The day-to-day work of the District Team

After an assessment of need and necessary authorisation, the main task of the social workers was to arrange the delivery of the care plans with one of the agreed providers. A review visit took place six months later. A second strand of work was the requirement to set up services rapidly on behalf of the hospital for 'Band One' cases. These were patients with a terminal illness sent home from hospital for the last weeks of their lives. A third area of work was the provision of temporary accommodation for destitute people with a health issue who had 'no recourse' to public funds.[1] This was time consuming and contentious.

The District Team was effective despite difficult working conditions. There was an acute staff shortage, and a lack of supervision. Annie, the operations manager who was also Andy's deputy, was on maternity leave along with one of the three senior social workers. The team's carefully managed staffing budget had been given to the 'children and families' department so there could be no replacement for her. Little thought was given to how the open-plan office layout affected the ability to hold confidential telephone conversations, or where to create space for sensitive discussions.

## The District Team's support for service users

Some service users had long-term conditions that affected their cognitive and emotional thinking, such as multiple sclerosis, Parkinson's disease, or brain injury through accident or alcohol. Others were physically and mentally dependent and at risk of exploitation or abuse from family members or carers. Hence the primary task of the team was seen as 'thinking for others'.

---

### Theo – the complexity of having to think for others

'In this case my client, Sheila, is 62 years old and had to go into hospital. While she was there her nephew Johnny, aged 17, moved into her flat and has taken it over. She didn't want to go back there, so I managed to get her a place in sheltered accommodation. But her nephew, who uses drugs and all kinds of things, has destroyed nearly everything in the flat so there is nothing for her to take to her new place.

So I'll try and get some cheap furnishings from the Shaftesbury Society. What has he done with all her clothes? That's what I'll be doing this afternoon. She's very tearful because she's scared of him and doesn't want him to know where she is. Her brother and his wife say Johnny is a good boy and she's the alcoholic. It's her flat but they have taken an injunction out against her coming round. I went there once with one of my colleagues – there were four young men there staying up all night playing music while Sheila said she was being tortured by the whole situation.

I'm a bit disappointed with the police because Sheila got in touch with them and they said it was a civil matter – I thought they were there to protect the innocent. She says these guys are there without her consent. She wants him out. It's possible that Johnny is an informant – Sheila thinks he is, but I won't get involved with that.'

---

Service users with borderline personality disorders had problems in thinking. They often had difficulties in establishing and maintaining reciprocal relationships with neighbours, family and agency staff. This showed itself through an avoidance of close relationships or, alternatively, as an anxious attachment, dominated by wild swings of love and hate toward those closest to them. Mrs Y in the earlier story was probably such a client – making suicide threats to put pressure on the duty senior to find someone to collect her children from school.

The social workers aimed to provide an empowering and containing environment for their service users. For example, they provided help through home care or regular visits to a day centre, sheltered housing and aids to ease daily living. I was impressed by the care taken by Rich, the administrator, with a client in the last weeks of his life.

---

### Rich – supporting a client in the last weeks of his life

Rich, the duty administrator in the District Team was proud of the shopping service that they provided for 'Band One' cases – those sent home for the last weeks of their life. 'If people are too weak to do their shopping like Mr S and they are in the latter stages of their life then they deserve the service. It's good to give a bit of help – and limit suffering.'

---

I was uncertain if counselling help for a service user was included in the social work task and if the emotional aspects of physical problems met current 'eligibility criteria' – for example, for a carer to gain understanding of the way forward with a disabled partner. However, during interviews social workers made it clear they thought their service users were helped by such a combination of practical and emotional support. They were gratified to gain the trust of a service user who had been hard to engage, and to be able to implement a life-changing plan.

---

### Clients who benefited from the District Team's support

- Dominic had been working with an isolated alcoholic over the previous year: 'His mother wrote that after he went to spend Christmas with them, they had seen a very nice change in him; so that made me feel very good'.
- Hazel was pleased with this outcome: 'I had a man who was very aggressive with a head injury. He was difficult to engage with because he disliked social workers. I had to work through this and it was very rewarding. I got him a place in a home where he has managed to settle and that gave me quite a lift.'

---

This practical emphasis on movement and throughput was perhaps in unconscious contrast to the situations of their service users, who were more likely to be drifting, stuck or declining. It delivered government policy with its emphasis on speedily completed assessments of care management. This allowed the social services department to produce the required statistical outcomes for the community and the Department of Health.

### The pressure of referrals

The District Team had inherited 250 cases of unallocated work when the adult services were restructured three years earlier. It had proved hard to clear this completely. They invested considerable resources in the duty system as a bulwark against the feared flood. After Annie left, Andy delegated the responsibility for allocating new work to Sonia, the recently appointed team leader. This coincided with a failure in the IT system. The team leader had to keep a manual record of all the cases to 'make sure nothing is lurking in the cupboard – we must prioritise the basket; we cannot leave cases lurking in there that could create problems for us'.

She held sole responsibility for all the incoming work and had developed rigid systems to keep control of the work and avoid the feeling of being swept away in the rush of cases. She was particularly anxious that initial assessments should be accurate to reduce the incidence of fraudulent claims. All questions on the assessment form had to be asked in the first meeting, even if completed earlier by the referrer and duty screener. This impacted on the social work staff, where the lack of discretion contributed to their sense of impotence.

Her working day was dominated by the pressure of referrals. When asked if anything good was happening, she noted that three workers had taken on some extra new cases to help her through the holiday period. Her situation highlighted the lack of mental space for discussion. She had lost a supportive supervisor in Annie and the prospect of management training. There was no space to consider alternative ways of organising the new work. The team used denial as a defence against the worry of their staff shortage. Annie's office remained unoccupied, as if she was still there, in spite of pressure for quiet space. When asked who was in her team, surprisingly Sonia listed six names even though four had either left or were on long-term sick leave.

## The emotional meaning of the work of the team

### *Fear of being overwhelmed by their community*

The team felt it was working with 'the grot' in society. The undertow of child trafficking and murder was evident, as was the constant need to be alert to adult protection issues. Family members were often implicated, and care workers themselves in some cases contributed. The team took seriously the danger of 'drowning' under a continuous stream of new referrals. They feared that the repressed negative aspects of the work might bubble up, like effluent from a sewer. Managers used vivid watery metaphors to describe their tasks, such as 'to keep the work flowing' and 'to unstick any blockages'.

The team had to confront and manage the negative aspects of human nature. In the depths was abuse of vulnerable and dependent people or instability verging on madness. Indeed, the team had to deal with 'the shit' in society both literally and figuratively. For example, a man was discharged from hospital before care services had been set up. He was found after the weekend covered in urine and faeces.

---

### Difficult service users

- Sometimes the service users, fearful of their situations and frustrated by their condition, were difficult to help: 'She is now ranting and raving and saying that she needs night cover'; 'Then you find she's gone to the town hall and been giving you grief'; 'He was really rather intimidating and scary'; 'He's a challenge because he is so demanding. Whenever we put in agency help nothing is ever right.'
- Occasionally care workers themselves were not above suspicion: 'We managed to get him into a house. Unfortunately he got too attached to his carer and he gave her a thousand pounds to buy furniture. But there is something fishy going on. The carer refuses to bring receipts!'

---

The activity in the office appeared to form a thick impenetrable surface, like ice on a pond or a heavy fire blanket. Perhaps it trapped the repressed and unattractive aspects of the work beneath the surface, reminiscent of a painting by Hieronymus Bosch. Was this where the negative projections were housed? Occasionally cracks in the surface appeared, letting some of the fears into the room – for example, when my neighbour exclaimed suddenly, while talking about an asthmatic service user, 'She might die!' as if she had just realised the risk. Then a member of staff told me that a rat had been found in the kitchen. The dirty and evil aspects of life seemed to be breaking through the surface, with only the members of the team shielding the rest of the community.

Was anyone keeping the social workers 'in mind', or were they working alone and unacknowledged? There are risks for social workers from dangerous service users. Incidents of violence and abuse within social care are not recorded nationally and monitored.[2] Councils rejected a proposal in 2011 for a national register of violent incidents involving social care and support staff rather than local reporting, but I can recall four social workers and two support workers who have been murdered at work during my career. It was not surprising that staff themselves sometimes failed to confront such aspects of the work when these were not investigated by the government department responsible for the service.

### The team's feeling of impotence

This pervasive fear left the staff with feelings of impotence. They felt impotent in the face of the mental and physical disintegration of their service users, the death of younger people, exploitive and unhappy relationships, financial restrictions, stringent eligibility criteria and the organisational restructuring to reduce two layers of management. Over the previous six months the team had a succession of pregnant women staff, unavoidably displaying an alternative world of creativity and independence from work. This had stirred up difficult feelings for the team.

There was impotence but also envy among those who would have liked to have been in the position of birth and renewal. This envy seemed to leak out into the team and limit creativity. No space was provided for the group to discuss and solve its operational problems. Sara could have coordinated the forms; and Rich, a skilled IT operator, could have set up a monitoring system with statistics and information for Sonia's new cases.

There was little identification of development opportunities. Andy's ambivalence toward the efforts of one of his staff to stand for parliament may have been an expression of his political views. But it may also have been the organisation's view of ambition. One day Andy was preparing a presentation for the Commission for Social Care Inspection. He was surprised and pleased that the assistant director had a whole afternoon to talk about adult care rather than the usual five minutes. But when I asked if he was going to present the team's work, he was quite startled and said, 'Oh no! Just the bigwigs do that!'

---

### The lack of delegation and autonomy was resented

'Many of us feel deskilled at the introduction of panels and not having any budget-holding responsibility while we may have to make a decision about someone's capacity or the need for a placement in an adult protection situation.'

---

Staff talked to each other after my interviews with them. Many of them had prepared carefully before our meetings. Dominic, who had been keen to make an appointment when I first arrived in the team, was determined to have his say. Before we had finished, the managers needed the room. Dominic barred the door, saying we would be five minutes. He then turned to me and said: 'You know you were asking about decision making? Well, we are not allowed to make decisions here!'

I had noticed that Andy would come into the main office for social contact and support. A couple of times he sat near my desk, and would sigh or talk to engage my attention. Like me, he was not welcome in the kitchen at lunchtime. This led me to feel that we were paired together by the team, perhaps as not belonging or perhaps I was seen as a substitute for Annie. During this phase Andy would talk about the concerns and demands of the job: staffing, inspections, piloting government initiatives, the poor government policies, commissioning services from multiple providers – and more.

He reminisced how in the late 1980s the senior social workers had introduced 'reading time' one afternoon a week. He recalled the setting up of a 'learning circle' where they presented cases for discussion and mutual help. This process reminded him of his earlier learning experiences from past mentors and from his peer group. He remembered a time of creativity and potency when a small group could introduce innovative ways of managing the processes of relationship work (e.g. case discussions). When I returned two months later, Hazel told me with pleasure that they had set up a regular case discussion group, and developed a plan to reduce noise by moving the duty system out of the main office.

## Summary

The District Team's task was to counteract disintegrating forces as their service users disintegrated in body or mind before them. This left an emotional legacy – a fear that they would drown in the work, as with a sudden heart attack, and the introjected impotence from their disabled service users. These characteristics had a major impact on their ability to operate in a time of adversity. The team's managers provided a supportive environment for the staff, but little mental space. The organisational culture, which did not encourage initiative, left the social workers unempowered to innovate or to make simple decisions on the organisation of their work.

Their service users needed 'keeping in mind', but the social workers needed help to do this. The employing authority and wider community did not take full account of the emotional impact of the task on the social workers. Even the regular provision of supervision appeared to have been temporarily lost – and consequently the mental space to allow a 'third position' to contain projected feelings.

## THE HOSPITAL SOCIAL WORK TEAM

The Hospital Social Work Team, based in the inner city in the same borough as the District Team, was located in the grounds of a busy 400-bed district general hospital, which had closed 60 beds to save money. The team consisted of 22 people and had their office in six small rooms above a day nursery.

Staff were required to arrange services for people no longer able to manage without help at home, to facilitate discharge from hospital – arranging alternative accommodation if necessary – and to free up acute beds. (See Appendix 2 page 135 for an extract from my record of a day in the hospital.)

The service manager, Mary, was in overall charge of the team and reported to Dawn, the principal officer at the town hall. The operations manager, Terry, managed the discharge process. There were two team leaders (Muriel and Liz – a locum) to manage and supervise four or five social work staff each. The two senior social workers, who had obtained the first part of their post-qualifying award (PQ1), supervised one member of staff each. In total there were four administrative staff – two of whom were provided by the hospital.

## Team of the year

This was a lively team, who used their team meeting to debate and discuss a number of practical and case-related issues. They had received the council's award as 'team of the year' and a photograph in the newsletter. However, I realised after a couple of visits that I would not obtain a realistic view of the work until I attended ward meetings. For this I needed NHS ethics approval.

I returned three months later to find several members of staff had been replaced and three others were still away on leave. Mary, the service manager, had gone on long-term sick leave two months earlier. She had come into the office that day but still felt ill. I remembered that I had asked back in the autumn what were her major concerns. She replied, 'Staff sickness and staff retention – we are all so stressed and tired, I don't know how much more we can cope with'. The team seemed to be drifting and lacked direction.

The hospital management's primary task of curing the sick was constrained by its budget. It was attempting to meet demand through faster throughput. This presented a challenge as the catchment area had widened in recent years due to the re-siting of two neighbouring hospitals. The hospital relied on the social work team to arrange speedy discharges.

---

**Mary's warning on the pressure to achieve hospital targets**

Mary had warned, 'I always say to new applicants "Forget about hand holding – it's a conveyor belt here"; we are always under pressure from hospital targets so I have recruited two locums to take up the flack [*sic*]'. I felt that her Freudian slip between 'slack' and 'flack' showed her feeling of vulnerability, and sense of being in a front-line war zone under fire.

---

From January 2004 councils were fined through the community care legislation[3] for each day that a patient remained in hospital due to the lack of availability of social care. The team's task was to expedite discharges for those who needed either support services at home or a permanent placement in a residential or nursing home. Councils were given substantial grants to invest in services to ease delays. The social work team had made good use of this, and recruited specialist staff: an operations manager, a finance officer, a housing resettlement officer and a discharge officer for the 'out-of-borough' cases.

Social workers had to assess the patient on the ward within three days. This included finding accommodation, writing a report and submitting this to the panel for approval – or be fined for patient overstay. Staff seemed to avoid personal contact, perhaps because they were worried as the lives of their patients appeared so distressing.

These factors probably contributed to the problems for the management team – all four managers left within two months – with subsequent loss of supervision and valued team meetings. This high level of attrition had a negative impact on the capability of the service. The emotional well-being of the team appeared to be temporarily neglected, just like that of the patients.

## Meetings to monitor the progress of patients toward discharge

The hospital managers held daily 'bed meetings' to keep a constant watch on the progress around the hospital. They continually pressed for local authority funded resources. For example, they wanted to use the social work team's 'step-down' beds (funded to hold people who were waiting for a place in a residential home) for patients with plaster casts taking up acute bed space. The hospital also wanted the local authority to pay for a new social work post for the short stay ward to make sure that people moved out into the community rather than into longer term beds.

## Multi-disciplinary team (MDT) meetings

### A distressing incident

On the way to the MDT meeting, I was confronted by a feeling of despair as we walked down the long 28-bed 'Nightingale Ward'. It was before visiting time, so all the patients were alone and silent in bed or on a chair. One old lady, like a little sparrow, brought her chair out so as to catch people as they walked by the end of her bed, repeating in the most concerning way 'Are you the doctor? I want to go home!'

What made it worse was that her cotton robe was open at the chest and I knew that I should straighten it for her. But what would I do when she clung to me – and would that worsen the situation? I walked on to the meeting room, upset by the scene and my feelings.

The team discussed service users' needs at MDT meetings. All wards held these weekly to plan the progress of patients. A number of different professionals could provide information, and work out together the best way forward for each patient. Each social worker covered one or two wards according to size and likely demand for care management assessments. The meetings appeared hierarchical rather than participative, and did not enable full discussion of cases. Also the administrative systems were not reliable.

Social workers had to establish their own professional authority with the hospital consultant and the team of staff on the ward. Two experienced social workers spoke proudly of times when they had intervened, telling the consultant that he should be inviting comment and listening to others, since this was a multi-disciplinary meeting. One affirmed, 'I'm not a person that shies away from asserting my professional role and also helping other people do the same.'

---

### Decision taken at MDT meeting led to family panic

As a result of major surgery Mr E had to be fed through a 'peg' directly into his stomach. He was discharged home with the district nurse booked to visit that afternoon and show his family how to feed him safely.

But his family became overwhelmed by anxiety as the staff nurse explained: 'His relatives got him home. Then the district nurse didn't come when they expected. They started to panic. They rang up and verbally abused us. When the Indian district nurse showed up there at 5 pm, they verbally abused her too. They said that they were bringing him back down here. They sent her away. They brought him here and we put him in a ward overnight. He did not really need to be readmitted. But that's the family for you.'

The hospital staff probably underestimated the alarm that his family would feel at taking on such a task without practice. If they had explained the procedure in the hospital, the family might have contained their anxiety until the district nurse arrived.

---

In two of the three meetings that I observed, neither the social workers nor other staff spoke. At one, the social worker warned me that she needed to keep her head down as she had too much work from her other ward. At the other, a newly appointed social worker, Gail, was on her own in the MDT meeting, having had no opportunity to learn the representational role through the observation of more experienced workers. I attended a two-hour meeting with her and eight allied professionals (occupational therapists, physiotherapists, etc.) when the consultant and junior doctor spoke about all the patients. No one else spoke. When Gail was handed six cases, she felt unable to protest. This raised questions on the effectiveness of MDT meetings, as well as the training and support available to the social workers.

### The emotional meaning of the work of the team

Philippe Ariès in his study of attitudes toward death refers to:

> The inhumanity, the cruelty of solitary death in hospitals and in a society where death has lost the prominent place which custom had granted it over the millennia, a society where the interdiction of death paralyses and inhibits the reactions of the medical staff and family involved.[4]

The dominant emotional meaning of the work seemed to be linked to the desolation and despair stimulated by the approaching deaths of the service users.

The team were in the midst of life and death issues. Inevitably there appeared to be an unconscious conspiracy to hide the truth. The social workers, like the nursing staff, found it difficult to work in such an atmosphere. They built up strong protective defences. The emotional meaning of their work had been shaped by two years of intense pressure as they implemented the Community Care (Delayed Discharges) Act 2003. The lives of all their service users were falling apart. People who made good recoveries did not need their services.

They no longer had the satisfaction of 'putting cases to bed' or 'doing a good assessment and providing a package of care'. The social work task was to hold together the physical and emotional aspects of patients while they were discharged from hospital. The care management assessments of the patients' lives and living conditions had to be based on partial and fragmented snippets of information like those mentioned in the MDT meetings, such as 'sister helps' or 'likes Classic FM'.

## The needs of service users supported by the Hospital Team

Service users in the hospital were faced with difficult emotional dilemmas brought about by their increased dependence. They often had to make the major transition from their own home to some form of residential care. The social workers were the only people likely to acknowledge the emotional importance of what was happening to the service users. But there was little space for this conversation as most assessments were completed over one or two meetings at the most. It seemed that the team's process of 'holding it together' for the service user had been reduced to the mechanics of assessment for a care package or submission of papers to the continuing care panel.

Sam admitted that he 'found it hard to get a handle on their lives in this rapid moving hospital situation; it had been much easier in the community where I had felt more in control'. The social workers were cut off from their colleagues in the community, who only made contact to complain. They also had little to do with the other social workers in the hospital who shared their premises but were involved in child protection or substance misuse. The emotional experience of working in the Hospital Social Work Team seemed as if everything was falling apart. Their social work task was to attempt to hold the show together, which depended on their ability to think reflectively about the task.

### Space to think

By the end of my placement in the hospital, I also thought the team was handling the workload in the only possible way – 'doing' but not 'thinking'. Anna Dartington pointed out the negative expectation in the 1980s and 1990s that nurses should not think.[5] The team were imitating this.

---

### Unexpected mental space provided for Mike by me as researcher

With few managers around, Mike used my presence to offload a difficult situation on the surgical ward: 'This man came in to have his arm amputated above the elbow – he had not visited the doctor and it had become gangrenous. After the operation the fingers on his right hand were discolouring. I couldn't get him to accept services – he was totally unrealistic. When I explained the danger of further infection, he became unpleasant and abusive.' He relentlessly described a second case where the patient had a leg amputated, projecting into me the same details of gangrenous limbs and disintegrating flesh that the patients had projected into him. Given the lack of any other space, he used me to get rid of his patients' projections.

---

## *What motivated the social workers?*

The social workers liked the intense experience, the throughput of work, and the sense that they would quickly become 'expert'. They were a successful team and had delivered the required discharges against considerable odds. But this was at substantial cost to their managers' well-being.

Isabel Menzies explains that we often use objective situations in our work to try to sort out our own difficulties.[6] When we are able to manage the objective situation, we can then be reassured that we are also mastering our internalised worries as well. There can be real satisfaction in helping vulnerable people to move from hospital to the community.


## Summary

The Hospital Team provided empty beds for the hospital by arranging care services or residential accommodation. It continued to attempt to make ethical discharges in the face of constant pressure from the hospital. It had to contain all the fearful aspects of suffering and death on behalf of the hospital. The team operated within strong policy guidance, was professionally trained and had a degree of support structure, but had little autonomy and the high workload reduced the opportunity for reflective space. They felt they were on a factory conveyor belt.

The social workers did not have adequate support to provide service users with the emotional containment that would have helped them to manage the demanding transitions and losses involved. Because the service users were already in hospital, no one helped them to acknowledge the loss of their homes by getting in touch with past transitions achieved – a process that facilitates a successful transfer (see 'Emily' page 29). The managers had absorbed the stresses and conflicts across the margins of two institutions and showed signs of exhaustion. The team kept up with the high workflow, but this strained their organisation and made it difficult to acknowledge the emotional content of the task for the service users or for the social workers themselves. The team needed creative space to rethink the task, and to renegotiate a more equal relationship with the hospital.


## THE MENTAL HEALTH SOCIAL WORK TEAM

The Mental Health Team was a specialist community mental health team of 18 people, including four social workers. The team was required to support the mental and social well-being of homeless people. The service users often had reduced intellectual and emotional capacity due to years of street life, drug or alcohol abuse, borderline psychosis, personality disorders, or a combination of all these factors. They could also be volatile and occasionally violent. (See Appendix 2 page 138 for an extract from my record of a day with the Mental Health Team.)


### The day-to-day work of the team

The team worked closely with an array of agencies focused on the needs of homeless people across two boroughs. There were about 130 clients on its books. Most referrals came from the street services' teams and others from neighbouring community mental health teams (CMHTs). All the clinical staff regularly covered 'outreach' sessions in the early morning and late evening, in pairs, to follow up referred people who were sheltering for the night. They also linked with an acute hospital ward, day services and a number of hostels. With the help of the information officer, they had considerable knowledge of a wide range of available resources for rough sleepers.

---

### The Mental Health Team in a tough environment

The Mental Health Team had a gritty front-line feel and sense of professionalism. It was accommodated in the middle of a dirty, noisy and somewhat dangerous district. This was illustrated on my third visit when a Securicor van pulled up just outside the office door with all its lights flashing. Its loudspeakers were broadcasting 'Help! Securicor driver requires assistance – call the police!' I saw the driver – rather dishevelled – inside the van speaking on her mobile. I gestured towards her but she shook her head, signalling she did not want help. The building seemed to shake with the racket and we could not escape this even on the third floor.

---

This team was the best resourced and managed of the three teams studied. Supervision was maintained on a regular basis; and valuable mental space was provided through team meetings and case discussions along with joint working. The administrators were empowered to make a major contribution. But perhaps through fear of being excluded like their clients, the social workers avoided exploring racial and professional differences – the acknowledgement of which would have strengthened the team.

The team had been established in the 1980s to provide specialist mental health services for homeless mentally ill people in order to reduce the number sleeping on the streets and avoid random attacks on the general public. One succinctly described their client group as those who are 'rough sleeping, borderline and psychotic'. The overt primary task of the team was to attend to the mental and social well-being of this elusive group, who had excluded themselves from society, but continued to create considerable anxiety there. The team occupied the upper floors of an old property on a busy road by a large railway station, in an area noted for its transient population. The secure entry was shared with a walk-in health clinic for homeless people on the ground floor.

The team's professionalism was shown by the social workers' sensitive understanding of their client group, and the way they adapted their interventions accordingly. Homeless people can be anxious that others will intrude on them with questions and searching looks. The social workers were sensitive to this:

> When we go to see some people on outreach, they won't even speak to us. Sometimes we don't even know someone's name. We just get to know them over a long time. There is probably an awful lot going on but it's all very kind of in the dark.

## Fraser – race and perception

Fraser was one of the four social workers in the team. His story of a service user illustrates the type of challenges that arose for the team:

'I have somebody in hospital and that's quite an issue really. He went to hospital with schizophrenia. He's a young chap, aged 21. There was quite a lot of aggressive behaviour which got physical towards other people. But it was in this context of his illness – and he did well. He's been in hospital for a little while, five months, which is too long and was really ready to be discharged six weeks ago.

Normally what would happen is that we'd approach a specialist mental health hostel and he'd be discharged there. He has quite good function skills – he has a lot going for him. He's a graphic designer and wants to go back to college. Unfortunately, Hostel X did not offer him a place, which is quite unusual. This was on the grounds that he was aggressive and things like that. That was quite a surprise. We hardly ever get our referrals turned down. We have very good relationships with them and most of our clients go there. So this was quite unusual.

He was black and it raised a lot of issues about race and perception. I went with him for an interview [Fraser is black too] and I thought he did reasonably well – no worse than most of our clients and that he would get a place. I presumed that it was just a formality but they said no. I took it up with my manager who has regular sessions with the manager at the hostel. I thought we'd get them to change their decision or look at it again.

So I wrote a couple of letters. I highlighted the risk factors and that he had been unwell. He had been in hospital for a good few months but has not got a history of mental illness. His behaviour is unpredictable, but with no past history, it is very difficult to make judgements. So we tried to give reassurance and said if he became aggressive we would monitor him and increase our visits, and if it went from bad to worse we'd reassess the situation. It is in his best interests to move out of hospital, and though Hostel Y would be more suitable, they don't have a vacancy at the moment. There is a new management team in Hostel X. We need to look at our relationship with them – this is the first sign that things may be going to be different.

They didn't change their minds so we had a big discussion in our team meeting about it. There were different perspectives about how to proceed. Some people said, 'It's outrageous and there should be another interview' – I was in that category really. Others said, 'Well he's not wanted and that's another argument' – I personally felt that we should not have taken no for an answer.'

## The needs of service users supported by the Mental Health Team

The Mental Health Team was known to be working with intractable and occasionally dangerous people. Many service users had borderline personalities, or could be classified as having a personality disorder as well as being psychotic. The team were able to give valuable support to these service users in addition to the food and shelter provided by local voluntary organisations.

The service users often had reduced intellectual and emotional capacity, and were described as having 'very limited empty lives'. This was probably due to living for years on the streets. The psychiatrist explained:

> The average life expectancy of rough sleepers here is 42 years. Around 50 per cent have drug problems and 70 per cent have alcohol problems. So we're looking at the extreme end of mental health with personality problems and social disadvantage.

Teams working with homeless people risk being engulfed by the projections received from clients and 'splitting into dismembered and fragmented states'.[7] Staff can be reluctant to confront their differences in a mixed professional group – for example, the Mental Health Team seemed to avoid any critical comments about each other even when these might have led to useful insights.

---

### Pressure from society to act unethically

'It's the way the media is felt in the organisation. Everyone wants to be blameless. No one wants to take any risks – but I don't like being risk averse and driven by this sort of blame culture – covering one's back. As long as you can justify your position and explain why you have done things and have a good rationale behind your actions, then you are not behaving negligently.'

### Pressure from new legislation

'You want to help her or do something, but really you can't do anything. I do feel it's a very discriminatory system. We are stigmatising them by giving them vouchers which identify them as asylum seekers. It is really unpleasant. I think the whole thing is very unpleasant. I'm sure they often feel persecuted.'

### Pressure from unrealistic housing policy

'One chap has had alcohol problems and schizophrenia for 25 years and we got him into a staffed hostel and he is a lot healthier and physically and mentally stable. But he is only allowed to stay three years, so we are worried now where to place him.'

---

### The emotional meaning of the work of the team

I observed the care and creativity that went into all aspects of the team's work. The warmth and nurturing was a significant part of their culture – with its ritual of fetching each other food and drink and their shared conversations. A team member commented:

You get the chance to do so many different things, such as support for other services and training. I think the reason that people stay is not just the client work but the team. We work very well together as a team. I think that people come back. There are quite a few people who have come back to work here. I think that is a real testament.

The working week was structured effectively both to keep the service user in mind and to provide space for the team members to think and reflect about the work. The office banter and friendships seemed to compensate for the bleak lives of the clients, and offered an important defence against the harsh streets outside. They also tended to be conciliatory toward each other and other agencies.

### Counter-transference insight

The following account of my counter-transference experiences shows the fear of a critical gaze felt by the team and by the service users.

---

### Feeling uncomfortable and intrusive in the group

My first observation visit was at the Monday team meeting. The team was discussing applications for a hostel vacancy, where one of the applicants was said to be violent and unpredictable. I found myself in an unpleasant reverie.

Rather than listening to the discussion, I was preoccupied with a difficult situation at home which had left me feeling damaging and incompetent. This stray thought of mine may have been a counter-transference experience[8] to give insight into one of the group's concerns. As I learnt more about the team's work, I realised that they were often concerned that they were damaging when trying to help their clients. They were preoccupied with the dilemma of having to act in a punitive way for the client's long-term good.

In the break Dave shared how anxious he felt with my presence at the meeting. He wanted to interject and put everyone's comments into some sort of context. He explained that Ed, the psychiatrist, often spoke frankly and he did not want me to get the wrong impression. I attempted to reassure him. But in retrospect it would have been more helpful to have acknowledged his discomfort. At the end of a visit I forgot my notebook. It was left among some papers on the spare desk. On my return I found an unsigned note slipped between the pages: 'Please do not leave this around, it makes us feel paranoid.' My forgetting the notebook and their reaction illustrated the persecutory dynamic in observing and being observed.

I endured several uncomfortable sessions of which my final piece of observation was typical. About half an hour into the meeting there was some complex banter and sharp remarks. I think Ed said something over the top about another member of staff – and people looked to see my reaction and whether I was writing the comment down. I felt intrusive and uncomfortable, and deliberately put down my pen. After 20 minutes of discussion Ed made a sharp in-joke about Fraser – the

*(continued)*

*(continued)*

only black social worker – that I missed. Everyone turned to see how I reacted. I said that I had missed the joke and put down my pen again and finished writing. The meeting came to an end. I mentioned that it was the end of the first part of my research and there would be no more observation.

The group eventually pressured me to give up making notes. I was unable to continue recording due to the intense feeling in the group. The group encouraged Ed to use his sharp tongue to attack me as the outsider, just as they used him to express their frustration with their clients and each other. Later, a friend asked, 'Have you finished your surveillance yet?' I realised that the word 'surveillance' precisely articulated the team's emotions.

What was all this about? Admittedly being observed is never comfortable. Kevin Healy points out, 'Being observed, especially if we are being observed in a crisis situation, may evoke the feeling of dread that what we are doing is wrong and will be exposed to the world for critical judgement'.[9] Only later did I identify my acute unease, feeling like one of their clients under a persecutory gaze.

The Mental Health Team worked with a group of service users who were more than homeless. James Gilligan notes that 'such people are made to feel ashamed, not only of what they do, but the deeper wounding of being ashamed of who they are – literally ashamed of their self'.[10] Observation was particularly testing for the Mental Health Team. I felt the full force of their hostile projections, in contrast to my experience with the District Team where the duty manager made an effort to put me at ease.

### Handling of conflict in the team

A number of clients behaved in a conciliatory way to ward off conflict. Unconsciously influenced by this, Dave the job-share manager worked hard to avoid or defuse conflicts with other agencies – 'It would only irritate the hospital if we closed the case now, so how about suggesting a case conference?'

### Difference of view in the team on handling a BME patient (see Leila's story in Appendix 2 page 140)

When I came in several times to see staff who had agreed to be interviewed, a professional conflict was rumbling under the surface. The psychiatrist and a community psychiatric nurse (CPN) were worried about the mental health of Leila, a middle-aged woman who had been sleeping rough for several months. Jane, the one black CPN, was deeply unhappy about their plans and finally confronted them in the team meeting. 'You know it's helpful to have a woman clinician involved, so why didn't you choose the only black woman clinician for the black client?'

This difference of view forced Dave to acknowledge the group's excluding closeness. But he missed the opportunity of siding with Jane, the black CPN, when together they could have made the case for reducing the statistics of compulsory admissions for black and minority ethnic patients.

The team's stable membership had many advantages in terms of knowledge, corporate memory and professional practice. But on this occasion it worked against recognition of internal differences. Race was rarely mentioned in the team, and Jane's feelings of exposure were understandable. Her overt 'softly, softly' approach was different from the mores of the team who said they talked through conflicting views on a case to reach agreement on the way forward.

Unresolved conflict was more common than acknowledged. Incidents of difference and exclusion emerged in interviews, relating to both personal and professional issues. Gill was unhappy that her social work student had been excluded from the monthly support group. She failed to convince her health service colleagues that a social work student on a six-month placement was in a different position to a nursing student on a six-week placement. Fraser was disappointed that the manager accepted a hostel's decision when his client, a young black man, was unexpectedly refused a place. Julia, the occupational therapist, disagreed with her manager on the benefits of admitting an older man into hospital for assessment. It was probably a relief for the group when they all agreed how poorly another team responded to 'no recourse' cases.

### Dilemmas in deciding support for service users

When I asked team members to talk about a difficult situation, each example had a dilemma to which there were no clear answers. For example: Would a mental health assessment be in the client's best interests? Would it seem punitive? Would the client disappear? Will hospital admission do any good? Should we just cover ourselves in case of a press inquiry? How will clients cope on a noisy acute ward after the solitariness of rough sleeping?

The team faced these diverse and difficult issues every day, and worked hard to provide as much cohesion and support for each other as possible. Their ability to act as a role model for other multi-disciplinary and interprofessional groups could have been enhanced even further if there had been more open exploration of their differences.

### Summary

The Mental Health Team worked with difficult clients with psychotic symptoms, borderline personalities, and personality disorders at the margins of society. The team was highly motivated with a clear legal framework. It was able to prioritise effort and continuously reflect on progress with service users, involving close interaction between experienced members of staff and those newer to the field. The team maximised mental space to work creatively and consistently with this challenging group, having clear boundaries for accepting work and managing their own staffing budget.

The team had good support structures and maintained regular and supportive team meetings. Its reflective and nurturing culture formed an important defence against the harsh environment of the clients. The challenge of helping service users often required the team to take difficult decisions in their long-term interest. All outreach work took place with a colleague – as did formal assessments. Working in pairs encouraged learning opportunities. The team demonstrated the capacity available in the front line if adequate mental space is provided for creative thinking and reflection.

## Notes

1  NRPF Network. March 2011. 'Social services support to people with no recourse to public funds – a national picture'.
2  'Violence against social care and support staff'". Published by Skills for Care. November 2013. pp. 9–10.
3  The Community Care (Delayed Discharges etc.) Act 2003.
4  Ariès, P. 1976. *Western attitudes toward death: from the Middle Ages to the present.* Baltimore, MD: Johns Hopkins University Press.
5  Dartington, A. 1994. 'Where angels fear to tread: idealism, despondency and inhibition of thought in hospital nursing'. In: A. Obholzer and V.Z. Roberts (eds), *The unconscious at work.* London: Routledge.
6  Menzies, I. 1970. *The functioning of social systems as a defence against anxiety.* London: Tavistock Institute of Human Relations.
7  Adlam, J. and Scanlon, C. 2005. 'Personality disorder and homelessness: membership and "unhoused minds" in forensic settings'. *Group Analysis* 38(3): 452–466.
8  Ogden, T. 1982. *Projective identification and psychotherapeutic technique.* New York: Jason Aronson.
9  Healy, K. 1999. 'Clinical audit and conflict'. In: R. Davenhill and M. Patrick (eds), *Rethinking clinical audit.* London: Routledge.
10 Gilligan, J. 1996. *Violence: reflections on our deadliest epidemic.* London: Jessica Kingsley.

# 5

# METHODOLOGY USED TO STUDY THE THREE TEAMS

## The support environment needed for a social work team

My experience as a manager indicated that successful teams need a supportive environment with five factors:

1 clear local procedures based on national legislation and guidance;
2 good management support structures and leadership;
3 well-qualified staff with encouragement of continuous learning by management;
4 sensible delegation of decision-taking responsibility and autonomy to social workers;
5 a reflective environment with supervision to help plan interventions for service users.

During my career I benefited from wider organisational experience and learnt how the different parts of a social services department interact together – and what people thought about their jobs, their clients and their managers (and vice versa). I grasped the interrelationship with other partner organisations such as the police, the hospital and community health services – and also the education system for school children as well as higher education for the professional development of all staff.

I spent six years on national negotiation of training standards. This was a great opportunity to find out what was going on in Scotland, Wales and Northern Ireland as well as England. I saw at first-hand how social work teams in different parts of the UK grapple with similar problems to high professional standards, and had endless surprises including:

• a foster carer who got up at 5 am and travelled the length of the country to share his views with our training group because no one had ever asked him before;
• the confused reaction of a Scot when asked about a child's 'heritage' – which had inadvertently conjured up the image of a 'stately' home, and a complete misunderstanding.

I also learnt from teaching and researching at the Tavistock Clinic about the unconscious processes that are evident in social work organisations dealing with grim client cases, such as child deaths. Social workers have to contend with massive issues of guilt and projection from clients. There are also wider organisational behaviours, associated with these painful and high-risk cases, that can lead to denial of the pressures involved and lack of discussion (e.g. filling meetings with routine minutiae and avoiding the real issues for the teams and organisation).

At times of major organisational change, there needs to be opportunity for staff to work together across newly merged structures, developing effective communication and referral systems – preferably facilitated by an organisational consultant to explore every-one's priorities, hopes and fears for the new venture. It is questionable whether sufficient preparation was made in local education authorities in 2006, when the newly formed children's services were established. Inevitably there was a risk that the new services – with their smelly, neglectful and sometimes cruel service users – would become the recipients of any split-off uncaring and unattractive parts of the education department.

Each time an inquiry about a child death is published, social workers wonder what they would have done if in their colleague's shoes: 'Would I have accepted that excuse? Would I have insisted on seeing the child? Would I have anticipated the worst? Who would I have talked to about it?' The Climbié Inquiry report was published when I was undertaking a doctorate in social work. The account of the squalor of the social services office was shocking – as was the obstructive and unhelpful administration, and hostile atmosphere among the social work staff. It was evident that there had been a lack of men-tal space for reflection. I decided to reshape my research to look closely not just at 'how much mental space is available for a social work team?', but also 'what is filling the mental space of social workers trying to help challenging clients?' and 'what is contributing to the positive atmosphere in one office, but not another?'

This was a challenging time for two of the teams as they were in the middle of a major restructuring of social work services into two different directorates. Resources were tight as budgets were being transferred to the new children's services. This restructuring pre-cluded a children and family team being covered in my research. In studying the three teams, I started by looking at the quality of their support from the five aspects mentioned above which had been important for my intake team and also my training and develop-ment team.

However, my experience of teams across the UK also indicated the need to look at the effectiveness of social work teams in the context of their own social services organisa-tion, as well as the wider interrelationships with partner organisations. An effective team needs to be part of an effective organisation in its widest sense, able to manage both the conscious and unconscious pressures and demands. These include the emotional needs of both clients and the social workers, with backing from the organisation to face up to some of the appalling cases and their stressful impact on staff.

Hence the five factors need to be seen as part of a system which is interlinked. For example, without recruitment of high-quality staff with good verbal reasoning skills, no amount of delegation and empowerment is likely to achieve consistently good out-comes; and without supportive management, a team will be severely limited (e.g. if given autonomy but insufficient mental space due to overload to be able to reflect on difficult cases).

As my research interviews progressed, it became clear that the five factors needed further breaking down, and their interrelationships identified. I found from my 44 obser-vation visits and 37 hour-long interviews that the teams and wider organisation needed to be sensitive to all the pressures on professionals. Awareness of the unconscious under-currents should form an integral part of the supportive environment for teams. Hence one of the factors in this framework is the availability of mental space for professionals and managers – and understanding how to use this space.

The following chapters 6 to 10 study the effectiveness of the three teams and their support environments based on the five factors in Figure 5.1, with each broken down into three sub-headings. The study does not indicate the relative performance of the

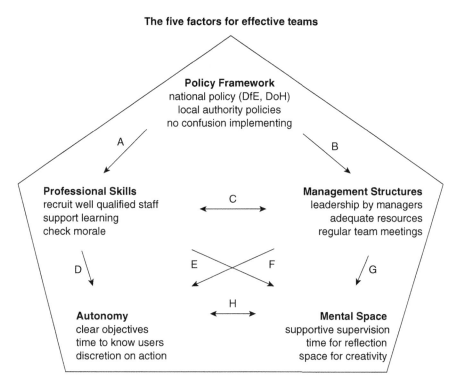

*Figure 5.1* Interrelationships of the five factors for effective teams

teams against each other in delivering outcomes, as clearly they had very different types of service users. That would need a different type of study focusing on, say, hospital teams in different parts of the UK. But it does show how different support environments impact on the effectiveness of the teams by enabling them to be well organised and empowered. It allows conclusions to be drawn on which of the five enabling factors need to be improved in any team. These are set out in Appendix 1 (page 128), with the opportunity for managers to consider how effectively their teams are supported in Table A1.2 (page 132).

## Notes for five factors for effective teams

Figure 5.1 shows some of the interrelationships between the five enabling factors. These are shown with arrows (some two-way) from A to H.

A: Recruitment and training of professional social workers based on national professional standards.

B: National objectives cascaded to help define required local outcomes. Also feedback to policy makers on problems of implementation of policies on the ground.

*(continued)*

67

*(continued)*

C: High-quality contributions to management and team meetings, speaking up about management issues and cases needing input from colleagues. Active management encouragement for continuous learning.

D: Understanding when to act on one's own and when to seek advice from senior staff.

E: Understanding the importance of reflection, and the skill of how to reflect under pressure.

F: Management delegation with clear objectives allowing autonomy through delegated budgets and discretion on time usage to understand service users and plan interventions – along with a performance-management system holding professionals to account.

G: Recognition by management of the need to facilitate time and physical space for reflection with managers through formal supervision and mentoring, as well as informal advice from senior colleagues.

H: Using mental space to promote the well-being of service users and to plan interventions.

### Summary of the five factors

The five key factors for supporting teams are summarised as follows.

#### Coherent policy framework at national and local level

There have been important changes in national policy over past decades. National changes in policy need to be disseminated to local providers in a clear and timely way, so the level of confusion and dilemmas is minimised for social workers, other referrers and service users themselves. There has been uncertainty at the working level on the implementation of past legislation, particularly if there have been complex restrictions on access to service.

At the national level overall policy is set by the Department of Health and the Department for Education. There will still be confusion for social workers on the ground unless the local authority develops policies and procedures to ease implementation – for example, how to balance the requirements for meeting numerical targets while ensuring the emotional needs of service users are met. Chapter 4 highlighted dilemmas for the Hospital Team working under pressure to free up beds.

#### High-quality professional skills

High-quality recruitment is essential. A poor appointment requires huge amounts of management time to rectify. Continuous learning needs to be actively encouraged so social workers keep up to date. Two of the teams had no budget to support further training, and staff had to fight hard to be allowed places on post-qualifying courses. Management needs to be attuned to the morale and motivation of staff, and work out what to do if this drops.

*Good management structures*

Leadership needs to be taken seriously at all levels from senior management in social services, to area managers, team leaders and all social workers responsible for staff. This needs training and good role models. Leadership includes the ability to inspire staff working under pressure, support a diverse workforce, encourage a learning environment, and provide supervision and mentoring.

Managers need to be able to communicate clear goals and targets, with realistic performance-management systems to hold staff to account. This requires regular management and team meetings, properly minuted with action points followed up, and staff encouraged to speak up and able to raise problematic case issues.

Adequate resources need to be allocated, both staff and finance, and targets adjusted if resources are insufficient – backed up by modern IT systems and administrative support. Much time can be wasted by professionals searching for information due to underinvestment in IT and communications.

*Delegation allowing individual autonomy*

Clear management objectives are essential – empowering social workers to take decisions in a timely way using their professional judgement.

Social workers need time to engage sufficiently with service users to understand their emotional as well as material needs. Cases need rigorous prioritisation – as the District Team carried out. The Mental Health Team was fortunate in having a narrow remit, though its service users were unpredictable and dangerous, whereas the District and Hospital Teams faced high workloads. Social workers need discretion on how to allocate their time and plan interventions – supported by delegated budgets.

*Mental space for reflection on the needs of service users*

The provision of sufficient physical and mental space is vital for reflection on the complex needs of service users. Formal and informal discussion between a social worker and manager is essential. There was a temporary lack of regular formal supervision in two of the teams. Time for informal discussion with professional colleagues is also important. Social workers in the District Team approached managers informally for advice, while the hospital social workers relied on colleagues who sat near them.

# 6

# THE NEED FOR A COHERENT
# POLICY FRAMEWORK

## Overview of national policies that the social
## workers needed to understand

Unclear or contradictory legislation causes organisational stress due to conflicting choice. Some parts of the law, such as the treatment of asylum seekers, can be discriminatory in practice, and may seem to conflict with the social work ethos.

The policies with which the teams had to work are categorised in Table 6.1 (high, medium, and low) according to case numbers, confusion, and impact of policies on the use of their time. The complaints procedures and concerns over adult protection were demanding areas for the teams. As shown, the District Team had two 'high confusion' policies to manage: 'no recourse' and continuing care; and four high impact procedures: complaints, adult protection, no recourse and continuing care (given the Grogan judgment see page 75). The Hospital Team had to deal with the high impact of continuing care decisions, but it was dominated by the high impact of delayed discharges legislation.

### Direct payments

The implementation of new policies inevitably puts an initial strain on the organisation, the service users and other professionals in the field. The implementation of 'direct payments'

*Table 6.1* Impact of government policies on the three teams

| Policy | District Team | Hospital Team | Mental Health Team |
| --- | --- | --- | --- |
| NHS and Community Care Act 1990 | HN LC MI | HN LC MI | Nil |
| No Recourse to Public Funds | HN HC HI | Nil | MN HC MI |
| Community Care (Delayed Discharges) Act 2003 | Nil | HN LC HI | Nil |
| Continuing Care | HN HC HI | HN HC HI | Nil |
| Direct Payments | HN LC LI | Nil | Nil |
| Adult Protection Procedures | HN MC HI | MN MC MI | Nil |
| Fair Access to Care Services (eligibility) | HN LC MI | HN LC MI | Nil |
| Adult Complaints Procedures | HN MC HI | Nil | Nil |
| Rough Sleepers Initiative | Nil | Nil | HN LC MI |
| Mental Health (Amendment) Act 1983 | Nil | Nil | HN LC MI |

*Key:* HN high number; HC high confusion; HI high time impact; MN medium number; MC medium confusion; MI medium time impact; LN low number; LC low confusion; LI low time impact had settled down by the time of my research. It was designed to empower people with disabilities to purchase their own help. Initially, the task of organising the service was put wholly on to service users. Frequently they and their immediate carers were too preoccupied and worn down by day-to-day problems to take on the additional demands of contracting and financing their own care. A husband was near to tears as he explained to me that caring for his mentally ill wife used all his energy, leaving him with no strength to arrange and claim for additional help.

---

### Direct payments created dilemmas for care management

The sense of social justice and fairness was often challenged. A social worker told me: 'When I saw her, she was lying in bed. She said she couldn't walk and was buying in all her services. Then the occupational therapist saw her getting on the bus. I asked her and she denied it. It's very difficult to say who are the genuine cases.'

---

Unsurprisingly, social workers became more wary of accepting people's tales. After some months the department had to work out how to meet the government targets for take-up. The appointment of a specialist direct payments officer was made. He designed a robust assessment system and enrolled a supportive specialist charity to help service users to manage their finances. By the time I visited, adequate resources had emerged, appropriate structures been put in place, and staff and referrers as well as service users were familiar with the procedures.

#### 'No recourse' cases

'No recourse to public funds' is a condition of immigration[1] that excludes people from welfare and housing benefits. There are certain exceptions for destitute people, children and adults needing care. At the time of this research there was little public awareness of this needy group.

---

### Problem of helping a 'no recourse' mother from the West Indies

One poignant case involved a mother from the West Indies who had joined her mother, resident in England. She was in her forties, employed, and earning enough to keep herself and her children. She suddenly had a severe stroke which left her immobilised and destitute as she had no work permit and therefore no National Insurance.

The social worker found that 'she and the two children and her mother were living on mum's benefit which was a pittance. The GP and I visited as she was not taking her medication. It was really sad. Where the children are concerned it really gets to me. I brought her some stuff down but there is so little you can do because it's "no recourse"'.

This social worker felt as helpless as the stricken service user, unable to fight against what she experienced as an arbitrary law. I was relieved to hear later from one of the locum social workers that she was actively finding resources for the family.

---

I was surprised to discover the amount of 'no recourse' work about which there was little information and no debate, such as the number of cases that the District Team held, and the hours that the team spent working out how to handle individual requests and deciding whether these met the policy guidelines.

---

### A 'no recourse' mother asks for temporary accommodation

I was observing the duty team at work when such a case came in. A 'no recourse' mother and two-year-old child had returned to the borough having been in a women's refuge on the other side of the city for a year. It took over four hours of management and social work time to reach a decision whether or not they had to accept her request for temporary housing (area manager 1½ hours, senior social worker 1½ hours, duty senior 1 hour, two social work colleagues who joined in the discussion for 15 minutes each).

---

'No recourse' seemed a demoralising purgatory between the heaven of legal asylum or residence and the hell of a forced return to the country of origin. Those with 'no recourse' included refused asylum seekers, people on sponsorship visas where the relationship with the sponsor had broken down, people who had overstayed their visa, and people who originally arrived in the UK on a visa and subsequently put in further representation to remain in the country.

The council was permitted to provide destitute people with temporary accommodation until fit enough to be deported, if they needed accommodation as a result of ill health, disability or age. This required proof of an assessed mental health need, or that they were pregnant or nursing mothers or adults with responsibility for children. It was an area easily exploited by some solicitors: 'The very difficult cases are people seeking asylum. We started to get some pregnant women – it almost seemed like some sort of scam. They all seem to come from the very same part of the world and we got half a dozen in a couple of weeks.'

---

### A difficult judgement whether a 'no recourse' family should qualify

Social workers had to manage the uncertainty of the legal arguments alongside the uncertainty of their service users' circumstances. For example, the District Team had become involved in a case with the education department. Some years before, a woman and her two children with no recourse to public funds had been provided with accommodation paid for by the children and young people team.

There was now a question that she had 'borrowed' the two children to qualify, as they were not attending the schools she had named. She might also be sub-letting the accommodation. Child trafficking had been intimated.

---

'It's very difficult when doubts have been sown in your mind. But somehow my mind tells me that the girl that I saw at the hospital was very different to the girl that I saw at the house. This is a horrible case. We are trying to get the police and child protection fully involved. It's very complicated. I definitely don't want too many cases like this'.

The council could either comply with the solicitors' demands or risk the case being taken to judicial review, which was an established way of developing case law. But the council's legal department had limited resources and was not prepared to risk the uncertainties of legal proceedings, which typically cost £30,000 per case. It was cheaper to concede the applicant's right to services. The in-house lawyers therefore tended to recommend the acceptance of the arguments presented. It took the social workers and housing officers many months to convince the council's lawyers that they should confront the clients' solicitors to avoid an increased amount of expenditure on such cases in the longer term.

### Staff told to implement stigmatising policy

The office staff were also repelled at the stigmatising aspects of the policy that they were expected to implement.

'It can be quite distressing. Although asylum seekers get a bad press, they don't get a lot of help – not as much as people on benefits. We had a case recently where a woman was given vouchers and these were refused at Tesco's. They wouldn't let her buy sanitary towels with them. So she had no money and it was clearly very humiliating'.

The interviewee was the third person to recount this incident to me. They were all shocked by the lack of humanity and common sense demonstrated by the supermarket check-out staff.

The Hospital Team was not affected by the 'no recourse' process, although the uncertain legal status of one or two patients was beginning to cause concern. But the Mental Health Team had begun to come across such cases among homeless service users. Though not supporting significant numbers of 'no recourse' cases, the team's lack of experience led to considerable worry and muddle when these occasionally arose, particularly given the possible exclusion of the clients from NHS services.

The Mental Health Team's criterion for providing services was whether or not the service user was suffering from a psychotic illness or possibly PTSD (Post Traumatic Stress Disorder). As the number of clients with the PTSD diagnosis increased, it was likely to be challenged by the Mental Health Trust. The staff thought that surviving rape, imprisonment or severe injury in one of the dangerous civil wars around the world was sufficient proof of the service user's need for help, if not for medical intervention. However, the legislation often prevented this. They complained that its repressive nature conflicted with their professional values – though as a specialist mental health team, the social workers appeared to have a little more leeway than other colleagues.

---

### A 'no recourse' PTSD case – conflict with professional values

When one social worker found that a client was not entitled to free health care or services, she was shocked.

'It doesn't make sense to me at all. It is very difficult. You want to help her and do something. But really you can't do anything. I do feel it is a very discriminatory system. We are stigmatising them by giving them vouchers which identify them as asylum seekers. It is really unpleasant and they quite often feel persecuted. The whole thing is very unpleasant. You think "Well, what can I do?"'

---

### *Delayed discharges*

The work of social workers and managers in the hospital was entirely dominated by the Community Care (Delayed Discharges) Act 2003. Under this legislation they were fined for each extra day that a patient remained in hospital due to the lack of available social care. The operations manager had developed an expert grasp of its workings, and the Hospital Team excelled at getting people out of the hospital before the deadline – by using 'step-down beds', setting up care services at home, or finding a permanent place in a residential or nursing home.

The delayed discharges legislation appeared well-matched to its policy objective of freeing up acute beds in NHS hospitals. However, it had unintended consequences. First, if patients were discharged prematurely and readmitted hours or days later, they were counted as 'new' cases with a substantial cost to the primary care trust's budget. Hence the savings were less than anticipated.

Second, patients were unintentionally objectified as the social workers avoided recognition of the pain and loss involved for their clients. They rarely had the space to empathise with the client's predicament and provide support when considering their situation. The emotions provoked by the need to enter residential care are best acknowledged – whether of sadness or relief at this time of loss and change. This can help patients to marshal their emotional strengths to weather the process.

Third, the Delayed Discharges Act stipulated a maximum of three days to make an assessment and to arrange a discharge date. This allowed no time to process the emotional impact of the work on the staff. While the social workers managed this through avoidance, the managers appeared to attract and collect the projected unconscious feelings. This risked illness and burn-out if not addressed. The service manager had left due to chronic ill health, the operations manager because of a personnel dispute, and the remaining team leader due to redeployment after a restructuring exercise.

---

### *Continuing care*

'Continuing care' assessments to decide who should pay for personal care were a constant irritant. The senior managers of both the District and Hospital Teams had to understand and implement the shifting sands of legal interpretations. NHS trusts and local councils developed criteria for a banding system. These were: Band One – needing total nursing care; Band Two – some nursing care and some personal care and living costs;

Band Three – entirely social care (personal care and living costs). Naturally patients with chronic illnesses assessed as Band Two wanted another opinion before their limited personal savings were absorbed by the decision.

There have been demarcation issues between health services and social care services in the community in the past. But the stakes for the vulnerable individual in the debate on continuing care funding were uncomfortably high. The government rejected in 2001 the recommendation for free personal care according to need by the Royal Commission on Long Term Care (1999). Thus care provided by local councils was means tested, unlike NHS continuing care provision. However, following a report by the Health Service Ombudsman[2] some care home residents were retrospectively awarded free NHS continuing care within the care home.

I was in the hospital at the time of the delivery of the Grogan[3] judgment on continuing care payments (see Appendix 2, page 137). Maureen Grogan's family challenged her local primary care trust's decision to deny her funded nursing care. The judge said that the criteria used by the NHS in their care funding decision had been flawed, and that Maureen Grogan should not have had to pay for her own care. It created a storm. In the densely worded judgement, councils were urged to reconsider their funding assessments. This required detailed attention by each local authority to unravel and understand the implications. It was another month before the Department of Health issued guidance notes on its meaning. Unsurprisingly, the minds of the senior managers at that time were filled with uncertainties on the funding decisions for the next 'continuing care' panel.

The principal officer, Dawn, explained to me that the only policy officer employed in the department worked full time on issues relating to the Department of Health's performance assessment framework and could not help. Hence there was no capacity to advise senior management on the ruling. No wonder she referred to a crisis in capacity and the need for 'more desk work from social workers' in case that created more mental space.

### Other procedural issues

In-house procedures based on legal and local requirements also absorbed a surprising amount of staff time, varying from 20 minutes to identify a correct form to up to two weeks to prepare for a complaints hearing. Cases where vulnerable adults needed protection caused concern to the District and Hospital Teams, and would preoccupy the social worker and line manager for a substantial period. Complaints from service users, some vexatious, also added to the District Team's burden.

## Conclusion

At the national level, policy is primarily set by the Department of Health and the Department for Education. Local authority policies reflect this in local guidelines, but there can still be confusion for social workers, for example, how to balance the requirements for meeting numerical targets while taking account of the whole person.

All three teams had clear national guidance and the legal framework was understood by the well-trained social workers. These had been agreed by the council and disseminated to staff. But the District Team found the implementation of 'no recourse to public funds' and 'continuing care policies' to be time consuming, as the procedures had not yet bedded down and agreement had to be reached on each case separately.

The Hospital Team had a major challenge in dealing with delayed discharge legislation, and interpreting the Grogan judgment on continuing care for particular cases – though it was less affected by 'no recourse' cases. The delayed discharge legislation achieved its objective of freeing up beds in NHS hospitals. This was fully understood and successfully implemented by the Hospital Team. However, its implementation caused social workers to feel that they were part of a conveyor belt. Patients became objectified and their emotional needs were frequently not met.

The local policies for the Mental Health Team to implement the legislation were reasonably clear and understood. But it considered that the repressive nature of the 'no recourse' legislation conflicted with its professional values.

Issues relating to the ambiguous interpretation of policy implementation often occupied the mental space of managers and social workers, particularly in the District Team and Hospital Team. This reduced the time for thinking about the actual needs of service users. The policies on delayed discharges were efficiently implemented but had unforeseen consequences (e.g. when vulnerable older people were objectified, leading to the risk of abuse).

New policies need more piloting before implementation to ensure improvements for the service user. Welfare policy in the UK has tended to be rather insular, learning surprisingly little from policies in other European or Commonwealth countries (e.g. the Netherlands, where there are fully qualified social workers in all of their children's homes).

*Table 6.2* Your part in policy implementation

---

*Understanding national policies and legislation*

- Review with your team the major polices that drive the work and identify where high impact and high confusion occurs.

*Understanding local authority policies and procedures*

- Are procedures for implementation of policies clearly set out and discussed?
- Can you set up a working group in the office to agree ways forward in implementing policies and procedures, liaising with head office?

*Avoiding confusion in implementation*

- Do you know how much time is wasted through lack of clarity on correct procedures?
- Do you know how much time your staff spend preparing for a complaints hearing?
- What role do you have in your organisation to see that the variety of procedural forms is reduced?
- Consider how best to reduce confusion (e.g. introduce clear guidelines and procedures).
- Should you lobby for a specialist worker who can act as a source of expertise on particular policies (e.g. direct payments) and make sure that their interpretation for the social work team is clear? Is there anyone already in post who would be interested?
- Are there particular local groups, service users or charities which might be able to help on the implementation of procedures?

---

*Table 6.3* Review the impact of government policies on your team

| Policy: Acts | Your team |
|---|---|
| What new policies are being introduced in your team? e.g. named social worker | |
| | |
| | |
| | |
| | |
| | |
| | |

*Note:* You can use the following abbreviations: HN high number; HC high confusion; HI high time impact; MN medium number; MC medium confusion; MI medium time impact; LN low number; LC low confusion; LI low time impact

## Now it is over to you

When you hear of a likely new policy issue, use the meeting with your manager and peers to explore the timing, service and financial implications of the issue. Armed with information, you can then share this with your managers or team leaders and together work out the timetable and action plan. Find time to consider the impact of current policies on the work of your team, referring to Table 6.2.

Use Table 6.3 to review the impact of government policies on your team. Consider current and new legislation as well as government directives, etc.

## Notes

1 NRPF Network. March 2008. 'Victims of domestic violence with no recourse to public funds'.
2 The Health Service Ombudsman. February 2003. 'NHS funding for long term care of older and disabled people'. HC 399 2nd Report – Session 2002–2003. The Stationery Office.
3 *Grogan R. v Bexley NHS Care Trust* (2006) Neural citation number: [2006] EWHC 44.

# 7

# PROFESSIONAL SKILLS AND DEVELOPMENT

Effective professionals need to be carefully selected, well qualified and committed to continuous development. Major investment has been made in social work over the last decade. Qualifying degree courses for social workers were set up for the first time as well as continuation of the master's programmes for postgraduates. Professional registration was introduced by the General Social Care Council, protecting the 'social work' marque. A hierachy of post-qualifying and advanced awards for continuous professional development was established.

I have found from teaching that, while writing skills can be learnt, strong verbal reasoning is a basic essential for social workers and should be an entry qualification. Eileen Munro[1] also came to this view in her analysis of what an employer can do to encourage good reasoning skills in staff, referring to the core knowledge and skills that staff need. Social work needs to recruit its share of good graduates and others with drive and interest in service users' needs. The combination of a decade of social work as a first degree and postgraduate MA courses is having a positive effect. 'Frontline', 'Think First', and 'Step-up to Social Work' are innovative initiatives allowing graduates to be recruited to social work comparable to the successful 'Teach First' initiative in education.

All of the social workers in the three teams had a professional qualification, varying from the non-graduate diploma in social work to the postgraduate master's in social work. Most of the social workers in the three teams were fully committed to professional development, and in some cases prepared to finance their own postgraduate training.

Table 7.1 compares the size and strength of the staff groups and professional development opportunities available.

*Table 7.1* Professional development in the three teams

|  | District Team | Hospital Team | Mental Health Team |
| --- | --- | --- | --- |
| *Staff* | 21: 3 managers, 14 social workers, 1 specialist worker, 3 admin. | 22: 4 managers, 12 social workers, 2 specialist workers, 4 admin. | 18: 2 job-share managers, 1 f/t psycha, 1p/t SHOb, 1p/t cons psychc, 2 f/t, 4 p/t CPNsd, 3 f/t social workers, 1 f/t OTe, 3 admin. |
| *Empowered* | 15 | 12 | 16 |
| *Chose to work with client group/team* | 9 Yes | 10 Yes | 16 Yes |

| Post-qualifying training | Yes, if keen, only one funded at a time | Yes, if keen, and could do without support | Yes, normal part of career, e.g. all 4 social workers were ASWs |
|---|---|---|---|
| Development opportunities | Limited | None observed | Yes – for everyone |
| Working in pairs | Rarely – only 'flagged' cases | Never | Often – outreach visits, assessments, etc. |
| Social work values | Yes | Yes | Yes |

*Notes:* a full-time psychiatrist; b full-time senior house officer; c part-time consultant psychiatrist; d community psychiatric nurse; e occupational therapist

## Recruitment and motivation

I was impressed by the effort that the team leaders put into recruitment in all three teams, and their ability to appoint high-quality staff. Leroy explained that he and Sonia checked for on-line applications several times a week. Although time consuming, this had proved an excellent source of high-quality applicants and appointments. So even under these stretched circumstances, there was confidence in the future. All of the managers in the Hospital Team were leaving for different reasons. But I met at least two strong senior social workers in the team ready to take their place.

The majority of social workers in each team were highly motivated and demonstrated impressive morale in a challenging environment, with considerable skills in working with people from marginalised groups. Their determination and enthusiasm compensated for a small number of burnt-out and seemingly detached staff. Teams were studied from several angles – for example, the proportion of engaged staff who had chosen to work there, who were committed to further post-qualifying training, who had other development opportunities, who could work in pairs, and who held social work values (see Table 7.1 above).

---

### The recruitment advantage for a team with good reputation

Several social workers had left unsatisfactory posts specifically to join the District Team: 'My manager refused to allow me to apply for the PQ (post-qualifying) course, so the next day I handed in my notice. I had a huge mortgage and two children and thought "Damn, what have I done?" Then I had an interview here and joined straight away. The good news is that I have more autonomy here and can get on with my job.'

Another social worker said: 'I moved to X which was nearer home but I couldn't deal with the systems and the management style – I don't need anyone threatening disciplinary charges if I advocate on the client's behalf. So I handed in my notice without anywhere to go. I came back here temporarily as I was desperate to be with people who could appreciate me and see what I could bring.'

---

Everyone interviewed in the Hospital Team had chosen to work there: 'I'd never worked in a hospital before and I found I was enjoying it. I tended to work quite quickly. I liked to be busy and this environment gave me that'. The Mental Health Team had an excellent reputation and all staff had made a positive choice to work there – 'It's different, it's interesting and challenging – the people are very marginalised and traumatised'.

### Commitment to post-qualifying training

It was impressive to learn how determined some staff were to continue their further education.

---

### A District Team social worker's commitment to further education

'I had a wealth of experience prior to being qualified. I came in mature and had a plan. I had a developmental programme I wanted to do. My target was to do my PQ One training and then to get straight on to become an ASW. I processed all the bits and sent them to the university. I did it within the timescale. You must have a vision of where you are going or you can become pushed around professionally and in relationships with individuals.'

---

The Hospital Team was not the PQ priority group of the social services department. Social workers had to be highly motivated to gain access to the PQ framework. For example, Kelly, a senior social worker, had obtained her PQ1 through the department. But she was financing the second stage herself at a nearby university, using time off in lieu for short absences.

> I'm academically minded and I get on with it. I was one of the first people here to get PQ1. They don't support PQ2 but I have gone ahead and am already on the last leg of the qualification with a local university.

She found the experience stimulating. She was doing a research project into multi-disciplinary working, which she saw as the way forward for the hospital.

However, another social worker in the Hospital Team commented:

> My plan for the future is to retire; I have not got into the student supervision bit; I must admit that when I finished my training it was one of the things that I wanted to do; but since working here, though I still think it's a good thing, I really don't think that time warrants it.

Her initial aspirations had not been nurtured in the hospital environment.

All the social workers in the Mental Health Team had become ASWs for the first time. The consultant psychiatrist in the Mental Health Team had set up a postgraduate master's level degree course at the nearby university, which several staff were completing. This created a strong ethos of personal development, helped by the group's ability to manage flexible employment patterns. A large proportion of the staff had postgraduate qualifications, which added to the richness of debate and creativity in the group. In contrast, despite the determination of some staff in the District and Hospital Teams, there were only sufficient supervisory or financial resources for one or two people to undertake the PQ awards at any one time. Other social workers, however, saw retirement rather than continuous professional development as their next step.

## Development opportunities

Continual professional learning is essential and has been developed over the last two decades, reaffirmed by the Social Work Reform Board, the Munro Review[2] and by the Office of the Chief Social Worker. The 'Knowledge and Skills Statements for Practice Leaders and Practice Supervisors'[3] recognises the 'depth' of skills of emotional intelligence needed in supervision.

Given my background in staff development and training, I was surprised to observe the limited approach to staff development in the work place in both the District and the Hospital Teams. In-house development opportunities can be valuable for all levels of social work staff – for example, encouraging area managers to make presentations to government inspectors, and asking social workers to set up interdisciplinary project groups.

This was probably due to the challenging situation for the senior management team which was splitting the social services department – with 'children and families' transferring to the education department along with a dowry of training funds, and adult services to the 'leisure and recreation' department. At the same time, there was an internal restructuring exercise with early retirement of some staff. So this was an exceptionally demanding period.

### Development opportunities in the District Team

The departmental management team did not seem to encourage on-the-job development opportunities for a wide range of staff. It was not clear how much supervision and development opportunity was open to the area manager. The principal officer was immersed in the politics of the reorganisation, and the need to interpret new legal guidance on payments. This reorganisation was not a good environment to encourage the bright young administrator in the District Team to develop an IT programme to monitor referrals, nor to coach the manager to present the team's work to representatives of the Department of Health. It was good to see that the team had taken some initiative and set up a monthly learning forum where the senior social workers invited different representatives from the community to discuss their work, leading to interesting debate and knowledge sharing.

### Development opportunities in the Hospital Team

The Hospital Team appeared totally preoccupied with the burdensome process of effecting timely discharges. Morale had been excellent when I first met the team, but three months later had plummeted. Job security was threatened by the restructuring exercise, management posts were being left vacant while the senior manager was away with a long-term health condition. The operation manager's application for unpaid leave was turned down, despite two years of working flat out on delayed discharges. This may have been council policy but put out the message that personal initiatives were not recognised or rewarded.

The social services training section was still running training courses. Hence Sam attended a half-day course on bereavement and loss, which gave him confidence to engage with his older patients. Compared with the other two teams, hospital social workers worked in relative isolation from their colleagues on their separate wards. There were no opportunities for joint working, hence new staff members took time to establish working relationships with multi-disciplinary colleagues.

### Development opportunities in the Mental Health Team

As a specialist team, the Mental Health Team was able to have flexible employment procedures, with several former CPNs back on a part-time basis to cover duty. Staff took on different community responsibilities – for example, to liaise with a hostel and day centre, to be an advocate for the team and its service users, and to provide training for other mental health professionals and volunteers. The single manager post allowed delegation of responsibility and avoided the need for an additional management tier, which contributed to high morale.

The team was committed to continuous learning, and had a monthly joint learning workshop with the psychology unit. They presented papers in turn and led discussion. Staff enjoyed supervising students on nursing and social work courses, which encouraged them to reappraise their work. It also used staff imaginatively (e.g. renaming the senior administrator as the information officer and lead administrator). The quality of her statistics and reports helped maintain a good reputation with the team's commissioners and colleagues in the field. She had devised a presentation which explained the team's work so that any member could show to other agencies and colleges.

## Working in pairs

Social work teams rarely work in pairs to help induct and develop social workers. This is usually invoked only for potentially violent situations. The demand on resources would be seen to outweigh the possible benefits. But alerted by the liveliness of discussion in the Mental Health Team, I discovered the strength and support the social workers found in shared working. They did their outreach work in pairs as this involved visiting the rough sleepers early in the morning or late at night. Joint formal and informal assessments took place regularly. 'Two heads are better than one' seemed the accepted rubric. It had positive benefits as the CPNs and social workers gained support as well as expertise and confidence from this joint working.

They also expected their work to be transparent and scrutinised by colleagues. This allowed for an openness and acceptance of skills and limitations. It provided confidence and security in work with difficult people – for example, when the District Team duty manager sent a second worker out with the duty social worker. It allowed people to observe and learn different techniques and ways of relating to people.

## Learning from each other

The benefit for the social workers and CPNs of joint working with homeless people was a revelation to me. Social work practice would be much enriched if all qualified social workers could spend six months of their first year in employment as a joint worker with a variety of social workers. After six months, professionals are inclined to settle into their preferred way of behaving. Hence this experience is needed at the start of employment. Professionals would then be much better informed and have the opportunity to internalise a variety of valuable relationship skills.

## Shared social work values

Shared values were expressed across all three teams: 'These measures we are implementing have implications for future services. That is important to me'; 'It fits in with my values of social justice and helping people access services.' The importance of social work values was evident when social workers were faced with the challenge of undertaking work counter to their professional values, as occurred with some no recourse cases and delayed discharges.

## Conclusion

High-quality recruitment is essential. A poor appointment can require huge amounts of management time to rectify. Continuous learning needs to be actively encouraged so social workers are up to date. Management also needs to be sensitive to the morale and motivation of staff, and work out what to do if this drops.

The social workers in all three teams were well qualified and experienced, but the opportunities for further development and learning varied. There was no overall plan to ensure continuous learning within the District and Hospital Teams. Many social workers had come into post determined to complete the PQ award to improve their practice and career prospects. However, they found that owing to the restructuring, 'children and families' workers had priority for funding, hence they had to fight hard for the opportunity. Even so it was impressive to find a number who had not been deterred and had achieved the award. They had visibly extended their knowledge, and increased their confidence and ability to perform in an interprofessional environment.

Social workers in the District and Hospital Teams had fewer development opportunities in the day-to-day work. The Hospital Team social workers had no role model to follow when attending the weekly ward meetings. This exposed new inexperienced workers to the risk of being dumped with problematic discharge cases. They needed to learn through a pairing arrangement similar to that of the Mental Health Team.

The Mental Health Team were well qualified and had developmental opportunities. They were skilled in learning from each other through working in pairs. The team had high morale and was well motivated. It had more flexible use of resources as a specialist resource, designed to help keep the city streets safe as well as supporting the homeless mentally ill clients.

## Now it is over to you

The research study demonstrated that teams had high morale and output if their social workers were well qualified and actively engaged in further professional development. Table 7.2 shows how you can play a part in professional skills development.

*Table 7.2* Your part in professional skills development

*Recruit well-qualified staff*

- Are you or your manager putting enough priority and time into recruiting high-quality staff?

*Support continuous learning*

- Are your staff sufficiently skilled? List all the staff in your team with their qualifications, skills, and how long they have been in their current role.
- Do your head office and manager actively encourage continuous professional development? Are you pressing for this for yourself? Is there a target of at least five days a year of training and wider learning?
- Introduce a debate about continuous professional development for social workers, assistants and administrators. Note who has or is in the process of completing some development activity. Should there be changes to meet the new initiatives from the Chief Social Worker for Adults (e.g. the requirement for a named social worker for service users with learning disabilities etc.)?
- Introduce a discussion on development opportunities at work. Do people feel they have the chance to expand their skills (e.g. chairing a community project group; being a representative on an interdisciplinary group; sharing experience at a case discussion group)? What are your views? How will you present the arguments to senior management?
- Are social workers taking on different community liaison roles or internal representations?
- The specialist Mental Health Team had a policy of the workers going out in pairs (for health and safety reasons). The added benefit gained from open discussion and learning best practice from each other needs to be shared with all social workers. How can this be done?
- What is your policy for supporting staff on PQ awards?
- Are you providing opportunities for your deputies and do they also encourage their senior staff?

*Maintaining morale and motivation*

- Do you discuss morale and motivation in the team?
- Discuss in the group who chose to work in the team and who were 'sent'. Do members think the team shares common social work values?
- Reflect on the degree of engagement or detachment of your staff.
- Tell your manager about your discussions and the results so that you can jointly agree how to take these forward.

*Table 7.3* Professional development of your team

| *Staff* | *Your team* |
|---|---|
| Empowered | |
| Chose to work with client group/team | |
| Post-qualifying training | |
| Development opportunities | |
| Working in pairs | |
| Social work values | |

## Notes

1 Munro, E. 2002. *Effective child protection*. London: Sage.
2 Munro, E. 2011. *The Munro review of child protection: a child-centred approach*. Department for Education.
3 Knowledge and skills statements for practice leaders and practice supervisors. November 2015. Department for Education.

# 8

# MANAGEMENT STRUCTURES

Good management support structures free up space for front-line social workers to think carefully about service users' needs, while poor structures waste time and increase stress. These support structures include: leadership from senior management providing a sense of stability; clear objectives set out and understood by all staff; regular team meetings with follow-up action plans, and staff encouraged to speak up and able to raise specific case issues; effective use of staff and performance management; diversity awareness; and good administration (e.g. IT, information resources, statistics, etc.). Adequate resources need to be allocated in terms of both staff and finance, and targets adjusted if resources are insufficient.

## Need for leadership and stability in the management team

Leadership needs to be taken seriously at all levels from senior management in adult and children's services to social workers and administrative staff. This needs training and good role models. Leadership includes the ability to inspire staff working under pressure and encourage a learning environment – as well as setting realistic goals, supporting supervision, mentoring, and the recruitment of a diverse workforce.

A stable management team is important. Frequent changes of manager upset the sense of leadership and risk introducing uncertainty of objectives. This was an issue for all three teams. The deputy manager and a senior social worker in the District Team had recently gone on maternity leave, leaving a gap in the team. The pressures on managers were constantly changing, making these stressful roles to fulfil for long stretches. I found that the management context changed completely in all three teams in the weeks between being invited to observe the team and the start of my research. Despite this, every team still had clear objectives for their work.

---

### Loss and change of staff

Some 'first aid' help for the teams would have been beneficial during the organisational upheaval that I witnessed when the social services department was split into two. Facilitated mental space to discuss and reflect on the changes would have reduced anxiety and improved relationships.

---

There was no chance of staff replacements in the District Team as the adult department had to shore up the staffing budget of 'children and families' for the reorganisation. The area manager was in a state of shock when I arrived and may have felt he had to support the whole team singlehanded. This situation led to rather long unstructured team meetings and the abandonment of internal management meetings.

There were also testing changes in the Hospital Team. The manager led her team to win the award for the 'best team in the council' for their work on the delayed discharges procedures. But three months later she was off sick with a long-term condition, as was one of her managers. Though her deputy and a competent locum team leader held the fort well, there was a noticeable drop in morale.

There were also changes in the management of the Mental Health Team. The social work manager had only recently taken on the position as a job-share on temporary promotion with the original manager who was a CPN. He was having to learn his management skills on the job. While performing well, he appeared rather placatory with health service colleagues both in the team and outside. This may have been a positive strategy but concerned his colleague social workers.

## Need for regular management meetings

The District Team meeting spent much of the time passing departmental messages down the line, particularly on the organisational restructuring. The pressure on the area manager and team leaders allowed no time for regular internal management meetings. Though managing a couple of staff, senior social workers had never been sure if they were formal members of the management team. Hence they were uncertain whether or not to invite themselves to meetings. Without an effective communication channel, the team relied on individual requests to managers to learn about new plans.

At my first meeting with the Hospital Team, the manager handled the agenda expertly. She encouraged contributions from others in the group, helped the garrulous keep to the point and drew out quieter members. The meeting was focused, interactive and participative with debate and ideas shared. There was space for people to bring up general concerns – for example, a newly appointed social worker asked the group for advice on a case and obtained useful contributions.

---

### Case discussed at the Hospital Team meeting

A hospital social worker brought a case for discussion, asking the group, 'What do we do with a patient who says she is not happy at her residential home?' Colleagues made various suggestions of people to contact. But the social worker said she was worried that this was only the tip of the iceberg, for example the patient was not being taken to the toilet when she wanted to go. The operations manager suggested that the reviewing officer was the best person to involve. However, the social worker thought that the patient should move to another home. No one verbalised the social worker's fears of about abuse. Even the team leader, who was normally very sensitive, did not mention adult protection issues.

*(continued)*

*(continued)*

The hospital social worker did not respond to suggestions of help from the reviewing officer. Her solution of moving the resident would have helped this client, but not the other residents in the care home. I wondered later if this was part of the team's need to avoid exposure to the pain and distress which was evident in each of my three ward visits.

When I returned three months later, the Hospital Team meetings had been temporarily abandoned due to shortage of managers. The glue that the meetings provided for a fragmented department had gone, with staff working alone on individual wards and sitting in separate small groups.

The Mental Health Team handled their regular team meetings well. The whole staff group met every Monday and Thursday, first for an allocation meeting and then for a case discussion meeting. The meeting was chaired by all staff in turn. There was a set agenda and rotated role of minute taker. Competent chairing with prompt time management allowed thoughtful discussion, and encouraged good attendance and participation. Problems were routinely sorted out.

## Flexible use of staff

Both the District and Hospital Team were affected by a temporary lack of management staff. Social workers were required to focus on their core function of arranging services or discharges from hospital. Without this focus the District Team would have drowned in requests, and the Hospital Team would have failed in its task of providing the hospital with empty beds. Experienced social workers represented the District Team at departmental meetings on adult protection, young carers, and for clients with 'no recourse' to public funds. Some other social workers could have been given temporary roles to help weather the acute staff shortage.

The job-share managers in the Mental Health Team managed the team's relationship with its different commissioners – covering two local authorities and primary care trusts. They also oversaw relationships with the many voluntary sector providers, the police and the acute mental health facilities. Staff enjoyed the delegated support roles with all these partners. The multi-disciplinary staff group were deployed flexibly. Former staff, who were retraining in different professional areas, were employed a couple of days a week to fill the duty officer role.

## Diversity

The District Team was ethnically diverse and well integrated. Issues of disability, gender and sexuality were understood by staff. Both team leaders were black – one particularly experienced and reassuring. Occasional disagreements arose because of different attitudes to work, for example, some younger staff were irritated by the handful of older women who avoided contributing to office life and just focused on their cases.

The Hospital Team used specialist staff well and had made a great success of the delayed discharge project. The team was diverse in terms of ethnicity, gender and sexual orientation. There were enough talented people to step into the empty shoes of the old guard when the deputy resigned on my last day.

Compared with the other two inner city teams, the Mental Health Team was surprisingly low in diversity, having only three black staff out of 18 – all strong performers. During my observations, tensions emerged in the group with one member being particularly acerbic in team meetings.

---

## Diversity

The racial mix and high standard of professionalism in the District and Hospital Teams, and the skills and professionalism of the ethnic minority staff in the Mental Health Team, made me proud of the profession's progress in recruitment, training and development to promote equal opportunities.

I hope that the recent training initiatives of Frontline, Think Ahead, and Firstline continue to encourage an ethnically diverse workforce. Diverse teams are vital with talented individuals such as Leroy (a black team leader in the District Team), Kelly (a black senior social worker in the Hospital Team) and Jane (a black CPN in the Mental Health Team).

The knowledge base of the fast-track and the university-based programmes will need to be dovetailed as it is important that soft skills such as diversity and social work values are equally well integrated. It will also be important to maintain relevant bursaries for universities to encourage diversity.

---

## Administration – financial resources and IT

### Administration in the District Team

The District Team had a business manager who handled the finances for community care with the support of an administrative assistant. When the assistant left for her maternity leave, the business manager was already annoyed by the lack of replacements for the two staff on maternity leave. She bypassed her boss and appealed directly to the central finance department, threatening to dump all the team's invoices on their desks unless she was given permission to recruit to the post. She won, but the area manager had to sort out the repercussions with his manager.

The District Team made good use of its two administrative assistants. They took turns to take all incoming calls to the duty team, expertly diverting those deemed irrelevant and completing an application form for a social work assessment for the others. I learnt that the social workers had been concerned about untrained people taking the initial call, and so for a period took on this task themselves, but the social workers were reputed to be so short tempered with callers that the administrators had to take the task back again.

Unfortunately no one in the District Team appeared responsible for keeping forms up to date, either on the IT system or in hard copy. Staff wasted time searching for what they required. One of the administrators could have been responsible for updating the information, removing old copies from drawers and the IT system. This gap was probably the result of the deputy's absence as she had managed the administrative staff. One assistant was highly skilled at IT. He provided unofficial help for staff, which made a great difference. However, staff were confused by the frequently changing instructions for the IT records. This was an unnecessary distraction, as was the constant updating of forms.

---

**The number of agencies providing home care had increased the demands on social workers**

'We used to have two organisers who covered the whole borough but now we have all these different agencies and you have to ring around and sell it – "I have a lovely lady for you" sort of thing. Sometimes though, not so lovely!'

When the domiciliary care contract was retendered, there was anxiety that service users would be put through many disruptions and changes. It was a relief when most staff were subject to TUPE arrangements and continued in post.

---

### *Administration in the Hospital Team*

The borough had successfully invested preventive resources by purchasing 'step-down' beds in the hospital rather than facing fines for bed-blocking. Unfortunately there was one major problem – two hospital administrators had been seconded to the section, as part of the hospital's contribution to the delayed discharges project, but they avoided using the local authority IT systems. They appeared to confine their work to arranging meetings and agenda papers. The director or assistant director of adult services in the local authority needed to talk to the chief executive to sort this, but as the hospital manager was off sick, the remaining two managers did not have the time to arrange this.

In contrast to the District Team, the Hospital Team had no business support to complete the IT invoicing procedures and social workers had to enter every estimated payment. If they slipped up, colleagues in the district or older persons' team would complain loudly. These tasks added considerably to the overall time pressure. Staff spent hours typing assessment forms rather than being trained to use the tablet computers provided. They queued to send faxes from the one machine to the wards, rather than challenge the uncooperative administrators to do this. However, their specialist posts appointed under the Delayed Discharges Act worked well (e.g. a joint housing officer/hospital discharge post).

During my research, the Hospital Team had the least effective support structures. While support and advice were available on a demand basis, there was no management capacity to step back and view the work with any sense of perspective. The successful management of delayed discharges encouraged the hospital administration to sequester more local authority resources. There was no capacity to challenge the hospital on the working standards of its administrators. The team also had to respond to hospital reorganisations. When hospital discharge coordinators were superseded by modern matrons, the social work department was faced with a new cohort of health service colleagues to work in partnership with, and to educate in the complexities of discharge procedures and legislation.

### *Administration in the Mental Health Team*

The Mental Health Team made excellent use of the administrative resources. The IT system worked well and timely statistics were provided to commissioners.

*Table 8.1* Available management support structures

| Activity | District Team | Hospital Team | Mental Health Team |
|---|---|---|---|
| Leadership | Good team leader and area manager | Good team leaders, absent manager | Good team managers |
| Regular team meetings | Irregular meetings, limited agendas | Had been excellent, but collapsed | Worked smoothly |
| Flexible use of staff | Pressure as shortage of senior staff | Used specialist staff well for delayed discharges | Well run by job-share managers |
| Diversity | Well-integrated team | Well-integrated team | Diversity issues, e.g. allocation of clients |
| Financial resources | Lost budget to children and families | Hard pressed | Yes – able to meet demand |
| IT | Yes, in part | No help, as local authority system | Yes |
| Administration | Good | Poor | Excellent |
| Finance admin. | Yes | None – done by social workers | Yes |
| Information | No, always changing | No, relied on colleagues | Yes |

Table 8.1 makes a comparison between the teams on aspects of leadership, use of resources, and effectiveness of management meetings.

## Conclusion

The management support structures in each team directly affected the effectiveness of the social workers. All three teams had good managers and competent team leaders. Though there were clear overall objectives, there was considerable variation in the way these were cascaded. Some of the teams needed better chaired and focused meetings, in which social workers could participate more in discussion, with decisions reached and implemented.

In practice, the District Team's fortnightly team meeting lacked time boundaries, participative discussion, or decision making. When held, the fortnightly team meeting of the Hospital Team was well managed, reasonably participative and reached decisions. The Mental Health Team also achieved effective discussion and decision taking with their weekly team-cum-allocation meeting and their weekly case discussion meeting.

Inquiries into tragedies often identify the paucity of administrative support. Yet the extent to which these tasks preoccupy social workers at the expense of thinking about their service user is still not appreciated. The District Team had good internal IT and business support, but the frequently changing records system caused unnecessary inefficiency.

The Hospital Team had the weakest administrative and IT support. Team members had to enter invoices on the system without any in-house IT advice. There was insufficient management capacity to challenge the hospital on the working standards of its administrators.

The Mental Health Team's multi-disciplinary staff group were deployed flexibly. Former staff, who were retraining in different professional areas, were employed to fill the duty officer role – a boon for the team. This was the only staff group who did not complain about the IT system or the demands of record keeping. Their senior administrator had developed imaginative information systems to which they all contributed.

## Now it is over to you

The research study showed that regular well-managed team meetings were one indicator of an effective team. Table 8.2 could help you improve your management support practice.

Table 8.3 lets you focus on the available management support structures in your team.

*Table 8.2* Your part in improving management support practice

*Management leadership*

- Do you and your colleagues make a good leadership team with agreed goals?
- How diverse are you as a team? Do you consider ethnicity/physical disabilities/sexual orientation, etc.? Are your head office and your manager seeking to widen staff diversity?

*Regular management and team meetings*

- Does your manager go to the departmental meetings with the other managers? Does the manager put forward your ideas and report back?
- How often are team meetings held? Do you think they are effective? Is the chair role and minute taking rotated among staff? Is there a fixed agenda to help? Are decisions reached? Do all staff participate? Do staff bring up agenda items? Are action points followed up? If the answer is 'no' to any of these, bring up points at your internal managers meeting.
- Do you and colleagues meet with your manager as a group? How often?
- How do you respond to a bright idea from a member of your team? Share an example.
- Do you ask their advice on what to do when you are uncertain about team or professional issues? Why not try that?

*Adequate resources and administration*

- Is your manager pressing for adequate resources, financial and staff, and investment in modern IT and communications?
- How is the staffing budget handled? Does your manager have some discretion?
- Who monitors the costs of services bought in for clients? How?
- Who deals with invoices and financial records in the teams? Is this the appropriate person?
- Do IT systems underpin your work, or do you duplicate recordings etc.?
- Who keeps all office information up to date?
- Do administrative staff take a lead on different aspects of office work (e.g. information packs, forms, logging new referrals, statistics, IT systems, etc.)?
- Do you have proactive administrative staff?
- Do you have one person/administrator who could ensure that correct up-to-date forms are available on the IT system and in hard copy?
- Do the forms give information that you want, as well as government?

*Table 8.3* Available management support structures in your team

| Activity | Your team |
|---|---|
| Leadership | |
| Regular team and management meetings | |
| Flexible use of staff | |
| Diversity | |
| Financial resources (e.g. for staffing and training) | |
| IT | |
| Administration | |
| Finance admin | |
| Information | |

# 9

# MAXIMISING AUTONOMY

## Meaning of autonomy

What do we mean by 'autonomy'? Autonomy allows social workers the freedom to act on their own initiative. They need to be able to think creatively and bring a fresh view to the myriad different issues that people raise when asking for help.

Donald Winnicott uses the word 'creativity' to refer to 'a colouring of the whole attitude to external reality' and specifically contrasts creativity to compliance:

> It is creativity more than anything else that makes the individual feel that life is worth living. Contrasted with this is a relationship to external reality which is one of compliance, the world and its details being recognised but only as something to be fitted in with or demanding adaptation.[1]

In a regime of compliance, people do not use their critical and imaginative faculties when assessing a situation – or when devising a helpful intervention. Aircraft co-pilots are trained to use their independent judgement so they can intervene if the captain appears to be making an incorrect decision.[2] Similarly, the introduction of checklists in hospital operating theatres[3] is more effective when all staff present are encouraged to speak out to avert potential errors. Primary health care teams with a hierarchical leadership have a higher death rate than democratically managed teams encouraged to voice concerns.[4]

High morale among front-line social workers is helped by the freedom to make decisions.[5] A team will feel empowered when it has clear objectives, a manageable workload, and the necessary resources, including delegated budgets. An experienced social worker in the District Team commented:

> I may have to make a professional judgement to protect an adult from abuse but I am not allowed to decide if someone needs meals on wheels. That must be discussed with a manager or go through a funding panel. This takes away our confidence in making decisions, and that in turn interferes with the way we think.

---

**Marlene – using her professional autonomy to help a young black man**

'I had one client, a young black man suffering from narcolepsy (a sleeping disorder) from injuries sustained when he was knocked down by a car. When I met him, he was spending his direct payments on gambling, and had taken out loans to do up

---

his council flat. He worked on the flat all night and his neighbours complained. He was a big man – six foot five and athletic. He was really rather intimidating and scary. He got into a lot of rows. The police were trying to charge him and get him into prison. When they found him slumped on the floor of the supermarket, they thought that he was on drugs. They tried to arrest him and he lashed out at them. They charged him with GBH.[6] Then Housing wanted to kick him out because he was doing unauthorised repairs. They couldn't work out what was happening.

So I picked up all of the social work problems. I wrote to the courts and to the police to put it all on hold. I got him back into the specialist clinic for assessment. His consultant was still trying to find drugs that would work for him. I managed to help turn him round, despite his aggression. Then I managed to get him back into the specialist clinic for counselling. I talked to Housing and attended a couple of conferences with them. I said "If you make him homeless you will have to pick up the problem eventually. How can we turn this round? Why not put an injunction on him so he can't do any more repairs?"

Eventually we got him a personal assistant. He would say to her "Run my bath!"; "Go and get my meal and put it on the table!" I explained that the care worker did not come to do this *for* him, but *with* him. There was a lot of swearing and door slamming. It was a real struggle but we managed. A charity now handles the payments directly with the care worker and does the returns. He agreed to have visits every single day. It's been nine months now, so I think this was a good outcome. The medication is working and he is not falling asleep; he accepts his care worker; the counselling is helping; the police are off his back and Housing hasn't kicked him out.'

Without Marlene's lively sense of professional autonomy, this man could easily have ended up in prison, as do so many with mental disorders.

## Effect of government policy on social workers' autonomy

Following recommendations in child abuse inquiries, successive governments have required local authority social workers to comply with central procedures in child protection and preventive family work. The Community Care Act (1990) – along with the move to increase care management for older people and those with disabilities – diverted social workers to put increased effort into administration rather than relationships with service users.

The government's spending review in 2010 led to five years of cuts to local government budgets. Councils worked hard to protect children's and adults' social care from spending reductions, through efficiency savings and substantial cuts to other services. But both adults' and children's services face mounting levels of demand, driven by demographic and economic pressures. This has inevitably led to tight budgetary control with less discretion for social workers on the ground.

Innovation was stifled as social services departments were unable to afford the implementation of locally generated ideas. Only centrally listed initiatives counted toward the performance assessment framework. The financial crises increased senior management involvement with front-line activities. During my research, the senior management team responsible for the major restructuring of the social services decided to control the salaries budget of the District Team, to refuse maternity cover, and to require every assessment of care services to be agreed by a senior panel. This lowered morale.

The more anxious a social services department becomes – over money or procedures – the less staff feel trusted and able to act with confidence. When planning the implementation of major new policies such as the Care Act 2014, the managers of adult services need to ensure that effective budgetary control still allows delegated budgets for teams, so that social workers are empowered to bring their best to the job.

---

### The risk that legislation may reduce delegation and local autonomy

The Community Care Act 1990 required packages of care to be properly costed. Hence it seemed sensible to devolve budget responsibilities, including to the smaller geographical teams in the borough. The teams could then make more informed decisions on competing priorities than someone in the town hall. We arranged a three-day finance course for all team leaders through CIPFA.[7] Hence, there was confidence that they could do the job, with support from their local finance administrator.

However, the departmental management team got cold feet, and decided to centralise the budgets. Needless to say, this allowed a group to overspend and expect to be bailed out by the others. Social work teams felt a loss of discretion and autonomy, and were discouraged from working out what would most help their clients, given the uncertainty of defined local budgets. Instead of encouraging delegation, the Act risked bringing about increased control from the centre.

---

### Importance of clear objectives and performance management

Performance-management systems are important to bring clarity to the objectives of the social work task and should allow more autonomy and individual responsibility. These reflect both national guidance and local priorities. Regrettably social work leaders failed to influence sufficiently the national development of performance indicators at the introduction of care management. I suggested this at a divisional meeting in the late 1980s, but there were no volunteers. Consequently the indicators were skewed toward financial rather than professional quality objectives. For example, the length of home care visits was decided by the available budget rather than individual need. Being detached from the social work task, the indicators discouraged local innovation. Hence social workers became restricted to 'value only what is measurable rather than measuring what we value'.[8]

Performance-management systems were being introduced in the District and Hospital Teams. In practice the objectives left open questions. Senior social workers were unclear about the management roles they were expected to fulfil. They were also unsure how far to help service users with the emotional aspects of their physical predicaments, such as mourning the loss of their home to make a better adjustment to residential care. These were not covered by the objectives. Furthermore, frequent transfer of budgets over the head of the manager to other departments impacted on the agreed goals and objectives – and undermined the ability of social workers to take decisions with confidence and reduced their morale and creativity.

The Mental Health Team appeared to have a functioning performance-management system and understood the different professional roles of the team members. The occupational therapist, for example, shared her work plan with the team. As a specialist resource, the team worked with professional confidence and in a democratic manner.

## Time to understand service users requires manageable workloads

Social workers need to be able to allocate their time to get to know service users, to understand them and decide appropriate action. This is difficult if workloads are too high. Managers need to be able to control the flow of work at the team's boundary to match the type and quantity of cases to the effort available.[9] Managing workloads is vital to ensure that delegated autonomy is effective.

### Workload in the District Team

The District Team worried that it would drown in the work. Owing to staff shortages, team leaders had to cut back incoming work to avoid increases in waiting times. A team leader checked all referrals, which took 40 per cent of his/her week – and an administrator acted as 'duty screener' on the telephones. Leroy, the experienced team leader, told me that he would check his social workers' desks for forgotten or avoided files, pointing out that if contact had not been made in four weeks they were never going to start. I appreciated his proactive stance. I remembered declaring 'amnesties' in my intake team when social workers could produce files from the bottom of their cabinets, and we would decide in a team meeting how these should be handled.

But team leaders then had little space to think laterally, evaluate the current system or invite solutions from the team. They were also less available for other activities such as attending management meetings or formal staff supervision. However, this effort by management to manage the workflow and recruit locum social workers was essential to free up the social workers in the District Team. Knowing they had the confidence of their managers allowed social workers the time to understand service users and provide imaginative support.

### Workload in the Hospital Team

The social workers in the Hospital Team had a limited sense of empowerment, having to take on all discharges. Experienced social workers could offer alternative solutions at ward meetings and divert some cases elsewhere, but new staff members were sometimes given an excessive work load that seemed almost vindictive.

The timescales demanded by the legislation caused considerable pressure, with the requirement to assess home circumstances, to interview relatives and to produce a report for panel within three days. The discharge officer said of outlying hospitals:

> It's a hierarchy in the hospital. The consultants shout that they want acute beds. Nurses panic. Doctors panic. They don't fill out an assessment properly. They don't understand the procedure. They don't understand that to arrange a discharge, a social worker has to physically go to the hospital, assess the patient and then come back and do a load of stupid paperwork!

The preoccupation with discharges was not thought through. No one in the hospital collected statistics on readmissions, which were costly and frequent. A proper cost-benefit analysis was needed to establish priorities.

### Workload in the Mental Health Team

The Mental Health Team felt empowered as they were an additional resource, and had some leeway to be selective on the service users to support and avoid overload – being able to turn away anyone who was not both mentally ill and homeless. Admittedly I was there in the summer months when there was less threat of elderly homeless people dying of hypothermia, and consequent media embarrassment.

## Discretion to plan interventions

Well-trained professionals need to be empowered to make the best intervention possible. When asked about any case that had gone well, respondents in all three teams quoted situations where they had been able to intervene imaginatively to help their client.

---

### Jill fought for an exception to the eligibility criteria

Jill explained what happened when she successfully argued an exception to the eligibility criteria:

'Sue had agoraphobia and had not stepped out of her house at all for four years. She was in a terrible situation physically, with ulcers on her legs through lack of movement. I tried everything to get her to stand and walk. Then I got her to wear socks, helped her into the car, and parked right outside the shop so she could get some shoes. That's the only way I could think to get her out. That was six months ago. Then last week, I bumped into her out shopping with her carer; she goes once a week now. Isn't that superb?'

---

Social workers need their own delegated budget so they can take timely decisions on appropriate support for service users. Even small levels of discretionary budget can make a difference.[10] The District Team demonstrated this, and was often able to negotiate imaginatively with their clients despite financial constraints. Most of the social workers could describe a creative intervention that had been successful and given satisfaction both to them and the service users. Everyone seemed to have their own example of 'beating the system'. Nevertheless the social workers were concerned on the constraints to their freedom. They disliked the centralisation of budgets, which meant they could no longer sign off small amounts (e.g. meals on wheels):

> In other teams social workers have more freedom to make decisions. But here everything goes to panel. The manager makes all the decisions. That means one's expertise is not fully utilised. In some cases we should have more freedom – I'm made to feel so dependent.

---

**Empowering social work training officers through delegated budgets**

As a principal officer in charge of training, I was initially shocked by my feeling of isolation when on my own. The team felt as troublesome as a group of teenagers whose parents had split up. I arranged a session with an organisational consultant. She advised on subjects for consultancy support, and areas for which I should find a psychotherapist. She recommended devolving part of the budget to each training officer. This gave them the status and autonomy to negotiate and manage programmes for their allocated division. Morale was raised and the training officers felt empowered.

---

Social workers in the Hospital Team had the least sense of empowerment. The team had to take on every person who needed discharge, though the social workers challenged those whom they thought too ill to consider moving. The timescales demanded by the legislation − to assess home circumstances, interview relatives, and produce a report for panel within three days − could bunch to produce considerable pressure. Explaining discharge procedures to new health service colleagues seemed never ending.

In contrast, a Mental Health Team's social worker explained her feeling of autonomy to plan interventions, and the advantage of not having a rigid hierarchy:

> The work is very varied. It's not just about cases − we get involved with training too. It's a democratic team and we have a relatively equal say in what goes on. We all feel that we have an input. So I think that these things make it an interesting team to work in. I can't see myself in a team with a consultant psychiatrist in the lead, where I was just instructed what to do. It wouldn't really work.

## Conclusion

Delegation of responsibility, based on clear objectives within a performance-management framework, is essential to empower social workers to take decisions using their professional judgement. If caseloads are too high, social workers can feel drowned with activity, and unable to spend enough creative time with service users to understand their practical and emotional needs. Well-managed delegation, including individual budgets, allows more autonomy and discretion for social workers to decide interventions. It also allows better matching of the workload to the capacity available.

The objectives for the District and Hospital Teams were clear on the material needs of service users as indicated in Table 9.1. However, they did not sufficiently encompass their emotional needs. The District Team was concerned that it would be overwhelmed by the amount of work. The managers had to work hard to free up the social workers to have some discretion in the use of their time to plan the choice of intervention to help service users. The social workers disliked the centralisation of budgets and lack of discretion to sign off small amounts.

The Hospital Team was in the invidious position of facing incessant throughput and the need to meet targets to free up beds. Despite success in delivering its formal goals, this had an inevitable adverse impact on the team's feeling of autonomy. Given its more

*Table 9.1* Autonomy in the three teams

|  | District Team | Hospital Team | Mental Health Team |
|---|---|---|---|
| *Clear personal objectives* | Yes | Yes | Yes |
| *Time to understand users without overload* | Just about | Overloaded | Yes |
| *Discretion in use of time for interventions* | Some | Little | Yes |

specialist remit, the Mental Health Team had more autonomy than the CMHTs, and was able to be more selective on the service users supported.

## Now it is over to you

Research studies show that social workers can help service users to better outcomes if they have some autonomy and are able to think creatively. How can you give this to your team? The information in Table 9.2 can help you encourage staff autonomy, while Table 9.3 focuses in autonomy in your team.

*Table 9.2* Your part in encouraging staff autonomy

*Clear objectives*

- Are your staff clear about their objectives, and what they want to achieve professionally over the next 12 months? Who they intend to work with? What sort of experience is needed to develop their practice?
- Do you encourage delegation of budgets and check that prioritisation of cases is taking place to avoid overload and tragedies?
- To what level is power delegated to allocate resources to clients? Is it to the lowest possible level?
- Has the team discussed this? Have senior managers agreed? Staff may be able to agree among themselves which of their service users fulfil the priorities best rather than requests going to the panel. Perhaps they should have the conversation.

*Time to engage with and understand users' needs*

- Is the team overloaded? Should you and your manager be prioritising more of the team's cases?
- Is there enough room in their day for individualising service user requests or situations?
- Can you provide support if they take on a case of child protection or vulnerable adult?

*Autonomy to decide use of time to plan interventions*

- Can the social workers in your team plan and decide the use of their own time to plan interventions?

*Table 9.3* Autonomy in your team

| Measures | Your team's views |
|---|---|
| Clear personal objectives and review dates | |
| Time to understand service users without overload | |
| Discretion in use of time to plan interventions | |
| Agree what will be a successful outcome for target percentage of cases | |

## Notes

1 Winnicott, D. 1971. *Playing and reality*. Harmondsworth, Middlesex: Penguin.
2 Gladwell, M. 2008. *Outliers: the story of success*. New York: Little, Brown.
3 Gawande, A. 2010. *The checklist manifesto: how to get things right*. London: Profile Books.
4 Borrill, C. *et al.* 2000. 'The effectiveness of health care teams in the National Health Service'. Report. Aston University.
5 Balloch, S., Andrew, T., Ginn, J., McLean, J., Pahl, J. and Williams, J. 1995. *Working in the Social Services*. National Institute of Social Work.
6 Grievous bodily harm.
7 Chartered Institute of Public Finance and Accountancy.
8 Wheeler, W. 1999. A new modernity? London: Lawrence and Wishart.
9 Rice, A.K. 1969. 'Individual, group and intergroup processes'. *Human Relations* 22(6): 565–584.
10 Lipsky, M. 1980. *Street level bureaucracy: dilemmas of the individual in public spaces*. New York: Russell Sage Foundation.

# 10

# MENTAL SPACE TO THINK REFLECTIVELY

## Mental space for reflection and creative thinking

Social workers try to help service users – often with damaged personalities due to adverse life experience – with material resources and relationships. Innovative thinking is as important in social work as in other challenging professions, whether psychiatry or engineering. Another mind can offer significant benefit through therapeutic discussion or supervision, providing the mental space to reflect and think creatively to disentangle complex emotions such as fear, sadness or anger. This process enables the social worker and client to reach a clearer view on the best way forward.

## Sensitivity to unconscious processes and negative projections

Mental space is essential to develop sensitivity to unconscious processes such as projection. Organisational dynamics were clearly affected by the unconscious world of their service users. The District Team sensed the evil aspects of life simmering just below the surface, and feared drowning in the work and becoming impotent like their service users.

When a social worker in the District Team referred to a shocking murder which had taken place years earlier near my home, I could feel the underlying hostility in the remark – perhaps suspecting that I had some reservations about her practice. But it also linked to the nastier aspects of their service users' behaviour which seemed a significant part of the District Team's hidden world. I was convinced of this when a second murder on another social worker's caseload was mentioned later.

The unconscious echoes of death and disintegration were close to the surface in the hospital. Mike's excessive detail of amputations and gangrenous limbs shocked me, as did the sense of an organisation falling apart when the last manager gave in his notice. This was simultaneously reflected in my own life by the death of my elderly parents-in-law. The Mental Health Team compensated for its fear of being scapegoated and ostracised by the group – fear projected into the team by their mentally ill homeless clients – by avoiding conflict and creating a friendly atmosphere.

I found that each of the three teams shielded society from unacceptable aspects of life hidden in the unconscious, such as sudden mental or physical disintegration and death. Society needs to recognise the valuable function that social work teams perform in absorbing these frightening projections.

## Ways to find mental space

My study identified at least 17 potential ways in which most social workers could find useful mental space through (1) *formal meetings*: supervision; team meetings; MDT meetings; internal management meetings; departmental meetings; allocation meetings; case discussions; learning slots; team away days; consultancy; departmental training days; and (2) *informal discussion*: personal reflection; informal talk with colleagues about work; social interaction; informal discussion with managers; discussion with a friend or partner outside work; counselling/coaching/therapy outside work.

## Provision of mental space through formal meetings

Table 10.1 records a snapshot of mental space during the research study. It was taken at a difficult time of restructuring for the District and Hospital Teams.

## Supervision

The provision of supervision has been a key development tool for social workers. Social work best practice assumes that regular supervision sessions are held between the social worker and manager, where issues are discussed and resolved. The Social Work Reform Board recommends a 90-minute session once per month. Traditionally the three ingredients of casework supervision were monitoring, support and training.

However, demands for social worker accountability have increased the monitoring part of the supervision process. The regular provision of supervision to allow reflective space ceased to be the norm in the 1990s and 2000s. It has tended to become an over-formalised meeting, focusing on rational facts and statistics, giving protection against criticism if anything goes wrong but of limited value for social workers in their professional work. In the one team where supervision took place regularly – the Mental Health Team – the staff considered the supervision 'managerial' rather than 'clinical' or 'therapeutic'. Lisa Bostock also found that two out of the three 'children and family' teams that participated in her research lacked functioning supervision.[1]

Part of the problem relates to the time pressures of modern working. Studies note that knowledge workers in commercial companies are beginning to rebel at the amount of time they are expected to spend liaising with each other,[2] and the need to catch up in the evening. Many social workers would recognise this, having to spend evenings writing complex reports for the courts. This inevitably reduces any enthusiasm for precious time during the day to be used in supervision.

Fortunately, there has been a movement to re-establish the reflective third position of supervision, recognising this is essential for the well-being of social workers and for progress on complex cases of adult or child protection. But management needs to implement this more widely.

### *Supervision in the District Team*

Supervision was patchy, if not temporarily defunct, due to staff shortages. Managers met with staff for specific reasons (e.g. adult protection, a complaint or HR issue). In contrast to the availability of immediate informal help, the formal supervision system appeared to have fallen away. Sessions were supposed to take place fortnightly for newly qualified staff and every six

*Table 10.1* Opportunities for mental space in formal meetings

| Formal meetings | District Team | Hospital Team | Mental Health Team |
|---|---|---|---|
| Supervision | Said to take place but not seen | Temporarily abandoned | Yes, regular – mainly managerial advice |
| Team meetings for all staff in office | Fortnightly. No space to bring issues. Manager ran agenda | Fortnightly. Yes, space to bring issues | Weekly. Yes, rotating chair, clear agenda and anyone brought issue |
| MDT meetings | N/A | Held weekly on each ward. Social worker alone. Daily 'bed meeting' | Yes, all meetings were multi-disciplinary |
| Internal management meetings | No, unclear who attends; often cancelled. Manager at department meeting with peers | No, 2 managers met informally, and help from principal officer. Manager at department meeting with peers | The job-share manager attended CMHT* social care meetings with peers |
| Departmental meetings | Yes, adult protection, young carers, no recourse | Probably | Yes, network of organisations and hostels. All staff |
| Allocation meetings | No, team leader approached staff | No, social workers took cases from wards | Yes, at Monday team meeting |
| Case discussions | No, but begun after research | No | Yes, at Thursday case meeting |
| Learning slots | Yes, at monthly teatime talk | No | Yes, at monthly support group |
| Team away days | One held in first two years | Unknown, not recently | Unknown |
| Consultancy | No | No | Monthly team support group, consultant psychiatrist available twice weekly |
| Training days | Yes | Yes | Yes |

*Notes:* * the central meeting for all social care managers in CMHTs in the borough

weeks for experienced social workers. But these did not seem to happen, probably due to the acute shortage of staff. Sonia, a team leader in her first year of the job, had her first supervision since Annie left months before, while Leroy, the other team leader, had no immediate sessions with his staff arranged in his diary. Members of the District Team still regretted that they had not implemented the action sheet drawn up at the away day 18 months previously.

The mental space appeared to have been lost – and the third position that is needed to contain projected feelings. This denied social workers at all levels the opportunity for reflection. If they had retained this space, managers might have been better able to surmount the dislocation in the team caused by the absence of the operations manager.

### Supervision in the Hospital Team

When I first visited the Hospital Team, the supervision system was functioning normally. The departing team leader said she saw everyone once a month, and new people such as Sam more often. However, there was a considerable turnover of supervisors. Two of the social workers had had four supervisors in the last year or so. One social worker told me what took place: 'At supervision we discuss most things. I can bring up any issue on my caseload or from MDT meetings – such as adult protection training or any problem with the IT.'

However, as Terry, the operations manager, made clear, he and Liz, the locum team leader, had to abandon formal supervision in the absence of Mary, the service manager, and Muriel, the team leader. Supervision had petered out three months earlier when Muriel was on leave and Mary went off sick. It was formally replaced with an 'open door' policy to cover the staffing crisis. Consequently the social workers only received limited support and space to think reflectively about their work and multi-disciplinary relationships.

### Supervision in the Mental Health Team

The Mental Health Team was the one team where the supervision structure was well maintained. The managers enjoyed providing supervision. Appointments were included on the daily movements on the whiteboard. The team had made it a condition of the placement that I would not observe supervision. The expectations of supervision had become so high that people seemed to fear scrutiny and criticism for even holding a session.

Views varied on its value as a reflective process or mental space. The interviewees saw supervision as a necessary management tool, often describing the joint decisions which they and their supervisor made on their cases. But one commented:

> I get supervision which is okay. I get that from one of the managers. It is more managerial supervision and case management stuff. I get my emotional support from my husband and informally from the team. If there was something that was troubling me I could talk to the team. I don't necessarily need a formal forum.

---

**Supervision being used by managers to influence a course of action**

There was also a sense that the space in the Mental Health Team's supervision was sometimes used by the manager to assert authority, and to influence, if not pressurise, the social workers into agreeing a course of action. One commented on a client: 'He has been sleeping out for at least 10 years. He's very entrenched. There is nothing obviously mad about him. There are no obvious psychotic symptoms. He is not particularly depressed. He is quite jolly in many ways. He's very stuck. But when we were reviewing cases, my supervisor thought that maybe we should think about a mental health assessment because he is not getting anywhere. I don't really want to do that. I said that I am not really happy to do that. I do not see any justification to do that. He is just one of those interesting characters who do not really fit into any niche.'

---

### Other formal meetings for the District Team

The District Team made little use of formal meetings for mental space during the research study. Meetings set up across the borough on specialist areas were supportive for those who attended, but longer standing staff wanted a second 'away day' to discuss internal structures for managing the work. The space in the District Team meeting was largely taken by news from the centre, rather than discussion of difficult issues.

With few formal opportunities to discuss their work, social workers in the District Team valued the chance to sit near an experienced colleague, or to catch a team leader or senior social worker walking past. These were their main opportunities for developing practice. However, they managed to maintain the useful monthly 'teatime talk' which provided a learning space to share views.

### Other formal meetings for the Hospital Team

The Hospital Team had to rely on each other in the maelstrom of delayed discharge legislation and the collapse of the management structure. Without supervision, they were dependent on the team meeting. This was the only wider forum in which they could explore together how to develop multi-disciplinary relationships within the hospital and across the social services department. However, it could not make up for the absent manager in negotiating with the hospital hierarchy over accommodation and resources.

The effects of this professional isolation were particularly conspicuous at the MDT meetings. These were intended to share multi-disciplinary approaches and information needed to optimise care or treatment for the patient. But the participants appeared unaware of this. One of the three MDT meetings that I observed lasted for two hours with only the consultant and junior doctor speaking, while the other nine people sat in silence. The consultant did not invite contributions and no discussion was held or decision challenged.

The views of the consultant and junior doctor along with the action required could have been emailed to participants. The team members would then have been able to spend the time more usefully talking to patients. There was no social work management pressure to improve the performance of MDT meetings. Two experienced social workers told me they had occasionally encouraged the consultants in charge to consult all the professional staff present. Attending alone, new staff had no opportunity to observe best practice and adopt a more robust attitude.

---

**Need for interdisciplinary discussion**

The lack of interdisciplinary discussion risked the hospital social workers being unable to think clearly about the case issues and their task. The discharge officer described the mental effects of the bullying and coercive culture that had built up in other hospitals over discharges: 'You cannot make a system work by cracking the whip down the line – that's bullshit. You're just going to get resentment. People will be sent into a panic and won't work properly'.

---

### Other formal meetings for the Mental Health Team

The Mental Health Team had structured opportunities for using mental space, which was essential as the team worked with a demanding and occasionally dangerous population. There were three or four weekly meetings to discuss the challenges they faced. These spaces balanced the needs of the mental health workers for reflection, creativity, problem solving, and managing the projections from the clients, as well as satisfying the the needs of the homeless people to be kept in mind.

## Informal support providing space to reflect

Table 10.2 shows the opportunities for mental space that were used by each of the three teams, as note in the field research.

### *Informal support in the District Team*

Resources were focused on new work in the District Team, which enabled support to be provided for immediate problems and dilemmas. There was good informal management support while on the job. During my visits I often saw social workers consulting a manager in the corridor or by their desks. Andy, Sonia and Leroy were always helpful, encouraging staff to think of wider options and advising on approaches. I noticed that managers also made time to meet staff individually to discuss difficult situations, such as adult protection, fraud and complex complaints. But these were treated as planning meetings rather than supervision.

The two senior social workers, Tony and Hazel, were also a source of knowledge and help to those who sat nearby. But without an allocation meeting, no one knew each other's cases. There was less interaction than in my experience between people about their work – as opposed to social pastiming. For example, two social workers told me how shocked they were to find that they held most of the team's cases for the protection of vulnerable adults.

Staff absences on maternity leave or long-term sickness impacted on the team. Andy was proud of the monthly teatime talks that Hazel had set up. But these could not fully compensate for the lack of space to think about the work. There was no time made available for allocation meetings, group case discussion meetings, or space in the team meetings for social workers to bring up issues. My research study helped team members to think about their situation, discuss this among themselves, and they introduced case discussion groups. This compensated for some of the other stress.

### *Informal support in the Hospital Team*

I was told in an early visit to the Hospital Team that staff received most of their support from peer supervision in their offices. Again, on our way back from an MDT meeting, another social worker emphasised 'It's the support of one's colleagues that matters'.

*Table 10.2* Opportunities for mental space in informal meetings

| Informal meetings | District Team | Hospital Team | Mental Health Team |
|---|---|---|---|
| *Personal reflection* | Difficult in open-plan, noisy office | Probably | Yes |
| *Informal – work colleagues* | No, staff did not know others' cases. Did talk to neighbours | Yes, sat in small offices with 3 or 4 others | Yes |
| *Informal – social* | Yes | Yes | Yes |
| *Informal – managers* | Yes | Yes | Yes |
| *Office environment* | Overcrowded and noisy | Fragmented but quiet | Adequate |

The small offices encouraged peer group sharing. I often heard staff checking out practical matters like eligibility criteria between themselves. One social worker said, 'Although it's sometimes total madness, I feel that here we bounce ideas off each other and it is more stimulating as a group'.

When I first arrived, both managers had an open door policy for consultation. The team leaders and senior social workers were also approached for information. The discharge officer said, 'They are fantastic managers; I can't speak highly enough of them; if you go to them with anything they will help you; they are all very good people; they just let you get on with it'. The advantage, as I could recognise from my experience of managing a referral and assessment team, was a smooth-running day-to-day system but with little capacity for any critical reappraisal of the task.

### Informal support in the Mental Health Team

During the working day, the mental health workers regularly checked client issues with each other, such as new duty cases, work planned together for the future, or what line to take with another agency. There was informal discussion on the groups attended and the people seen. The team were committed to having at least two clinicians in the building at all times. This policy was for health and safety reasons, but also emphasised the shared nature of the work. The mental health workers went on outreach visits in pairs, and reached assessment decisions in partnership with another mental health worker.

---

## The Mental Health Team debated cases thoroughly

'You feel hard decisions are really discussed and everyone has a chance to say what they think. People feel free to disagree. It's good that the medical team and the nursing staff and social workers meet together and talk through things. In some other services the medical decision is final, whereas here it is more as equals and we make a team decision.'

---

The Mental Health Team successfully addressed these issues through their twice-weekly meetings. New cases were discussed, and old and problematic cases were booked in for review. This had been suggested a couple of years earlier by an Australian locum – and illustrated the group's openness to new ideas and creativity. It was effective because the meetings were well run. All the staff attended and contributed to discussion. They used these opportunities to think about and debate problematic issues. The consultant psychiatrist also attended these meetings, and staff consulted him individually on particular cases after the meeting.

### Quality of physical environment

The impact of poor facilities and attitudes in some offices has been highlighted in inquiries into child deaths, but this is still not taken sufficiently seriously. Eileen Munro pointed out the employer's obligation to provide an effective working environment:

The quality of the physical environment affects people's ability to function. It is harder for people to concentrate in noisy, crowded, unheated or badly ventilated offices. Adequate administration and IT support are also important factors in enabling staff to concentrate on the difficult aspects of their work.[3]

Research findings also point to the time taken to regain full concentration after short interruptions.[4] Switching from one task to another reduces efficiency while the brain lingers on the old task rather than attacking the new one. Noisy, open-plan offices, such as the District Team's, make it extremely difficult to reflect on what is happening in a case. The current habit of requiring staff to hot-desk even forces social workers to travel to other offices or use their cars as a workplace.[5]

---

### Survey confirms lack of quiet accommodation for social workers

A survey in Professional Social Work in 2015 had over 600 responses from around the UK. Results showed that 73 per cent of social workers said they had no access to a quiet place to work. It is short-sighted to train professionals to be skilled at reaching complex judgements but fail to provide appropriate space to think through difficult social issues.

---

Eileen Munro has also alerted employers to the downside of hot-desking[6] and consequent reduction in informal supportive contact for social workers to discuss reflections with trusted colleagues – which is also a problem with the growth of home working. Unable to share their concerns and test their assessments, social workers will take their anxieties home and risk burn-out.

### *Quality of physical environment for the District Team*

All staff in the District Team had personal desks and access to a sizeable kitchen with space for sitting and chatting. However, it had the most disruptive environment with no quiet space to work or think – an open-plan office with a bank of desks belonging to another department in their midst, whose officers usually had a radio playing. Yet they held disturbing caseloads, working with people their own age liable to be struck by sudden disability or death. The overall noise produced considerable stress, with social workers often unable to hold sensitive telephone conversations.

---

### The overall noise in the District Team produced considerable stress

One worker said: 'I have been listening to people on the telephone telling me that their cancer has advanced or their relative has died and people have been laughing really loudly next to me. Not only have I been conscious that they can hear the laughter but it has affected my ability to respond, to think through how to respond in a sensitive way.'

Nobody remonstrated, perhaps because the social work team were tenants and felt powerless to take charge of their space.

---

Quiet rooms could be booked downstairs in the other department, but the lack of readily available privacy seemed a disincentive against holding supervision sessions. Nor had this problem been thought through and the limited space maximised. While most people would use the area manager's office for phone calls or meetings while he was out, the deputy's small office remained unused while she was on maternity leave. I was surprised that the business manager did not use this spare office to work on her accounts.

I discovered that it had taken two years to move the photocopier out of the main office. The team had no means of making and implementing decisions. This inability to manage its working environment contrasted with the improvements which the social workers brought about for their service users. There seemed to be little nurturing energy left as this had all been expended on the service users.

### Quality of physical environment for the Hospital Team

The Hospital Team were seated in small rooms with four or five staff in each. There was usually extra space as much of the social workers' activity took place on the wards. These smaller offices helped them to form close relationships with their colleagues. Though not particularly attractive, the office environment was functional and each member of the team had a personal desk. However, I was never shown the kitchen or offered a cup of tea – while the toilets, shared with other tenants, were barely usable.

### Quality of physical environment for the Mental Health Team

The Mental Health Team had two open-plan offices. The job-share managers sat along-side their colleagues and the three administrators in one large office. A whiteboard showed everyone's appointments at a glance. Four of the team sat downstairs next to the kitchen, and each had a personal desk. There were two small interviewing rooms on the ground floor, where part of the NHS team offered medical care for homeless people. This accommodation was satisfactory as staff were often out on visits and were quiet when at their desks.

### Conclusion

Social workers need to understand the emotional as well as the material needs of service users – as now encouraged by the Care Act 2014. The provision of sufficient physical and mental space is vital for reflection on their complex needs. Formal and informal discussion between a social worker and manager is essential. Time for informal discussion with professional colleagues is also important.

There is often little time within a team leader's working day to be emotionally availa-ble for staff. In the teams I studied, this was partly overcome by informal ad hoc meetings between a manager and social worker. Though valued as an opportunity to reflect on a case, it could not substitute for the missing formal supervision.

Organisations want smooth-running systems with managers responsible for ensuring that the work is being dealt with in a timely way. However, the demands of audit do not provide managers or social workers with sufficient support to provide continuous engagement with troubled and troubling people. First-line managers need training in clinical supervision to gain the skill to provide a dispassionate containing space and, indeed, to receive this themselves. The government plans for new training for practice supervisors are timely as part of the 'Firstline' initiative, in addition to training courses by expert providers.

### The District Team

In common with other departments, supervision had become over-formalised and focused mainly on facts and statistics needed for performance indicators and case records. It was not seen as clinical supervision offering a reflective space. The main opportunities for reflection with colleagues and senior managers arose informally. There did not appear to be any regular training or developmental opportunities available for those who had to provide staff support and clinical supervision.

### The Hospital Team

The multi-disciplinary ward meetings in the hospital did not allow for discussion or a sharing of perspectives. The culture was hierarchical rather than democratic, with insufficient opportunity for reflection, discussion or creative problem solving. Given the collapse of the management structure, the two remaining managers could not find time for supervision and replaced this with an 'open door' policy to cover the staffing crisis. The Hospital Team mainly relied on each other for reflective discussion.

### The Mental Health Team

The Mental Health Team benefited from the structured opportunities for mental space with regular supervision along with democratic decision making, creative approaches to service users, a safe working environment and an appreciation of each other's specialist skills. The team also put high priority on informal mental space for the team. Being a specialist team they were able to manage the work flow. But having the most volatile and unpredictable client group (which earlier had included a serial murderer), they took great care to reach correct decisions on intervention. Other social work and multi-disciplinary front-line teams would benefit if mental space was given the same priority by employers.

## Now it is over to you

My study identified 17 potential ways in which most social workers could experience some mental space: through formal and informal meetings. Try thinking about the points in Table 10.3 and add your own ideas. Then talk to your manager and peers to get their inputs. Take advantage of some other initiative – such as a new policy – and try building in time for reflection.

*Table 10.3* Your part in encouraging the use of mental space for reflection

*Supportive supervision*

- What formal opportunities for reflection do members of your team have? Do you give and receive regular supervision/mentoring? Is formal supervision held monthly? Do team members see this as a supportive process or another exercise in managerial checking of progress?
- Ask your team to check diaries over the last three months against the list in Table 10.4 (or your department's equivalent). Note how often each occurred and when they have been able to participate. Share the results in a group meeting.
- Is your team missing out? Are some social workers always absent?

*Reflection with colleagues*

- Consultancy – do a number of people share a problem (e.g. dealing with domestic violence)?
- Could the larger team be more imaginative (e.g. learning lunches when someone brings and presents a subject for discussion)?
- Do you have regular lunch with a colleague for mutual support – and occasional group suppers with a larger number of peers?

*Time and space for creativity*

- Is the working environment for your staff conducive for reflective thinking – with enough space and sufficiently quiet?
- Can staff debrief with colleagues on return from an interview?
- Take the results and ideas on how to find more time for creative reflection to your management meeting.

Take two or three meetings to discuss which methods you and your team would like to use. Consider how often to meet and an evaluation meeting for each.

*Table 10.4* Formal opportunities for mental space in your team

| *Formal opportunities* | *Your team's views* |
|---|---|
| You and your staff group meeting? | |
| Supervision – one to one or group? | |
| Team meetings | |
| Multi-disciplinary team (MDT) meetings | |
| Internal management meetings (for you) | |

| | |
|---|---|
| Departmental meetings | |
| Allocation meetings | |
| Case discussions | |
| Learning slots | |
| Team away days | |
| Consultancy | |
| Departmental training days | |

Table 10.5 Informal opportunities for mental space in your team

| Informal opportunities | Your team's views |
|---|---|
| Informal meetings | |
| Personal reflection | |
| Informal – work colleagues | |
| Informal – social | |
| Informal – managers | |
| Office environment | |

## Notes

1 Bostock, L., Bairstow, S., Fish, S. and Macleod, F. 2004. *Managing risk within child welfare: promoting safety management and reflective decision-making.* Social Care Institute for Excellence.
2 *The Economist.* 23 January 2016. 'Schumpeter – the collaboration curse, the fashion for making employees collaborate has gone too far'.
3 Munro, E. 2002. *Effective child protection.* London: Sage.
4 Mark, G. University of California quoted in *The Economist* 23 January 2016 'Schumpeter – the collaboration curse, the fashion for making employees collaborate has gone too far'.
5 Professional Social Work. January 2016. Published by British Association of Social Workers.
6 *The Guardian.* 29 April 2016. 'Hot-desking increases social worker burn-out risk'.

# 11

# CONCLUSIONS

The study of the three teams shows how good support environments encompassing the five factors identified can help effective social work practice. Appendix 1 (page 128) and Table A1.1 summarise their relative quality in underpinning the effectiveness of the teams. This chapter draws conclusions on changes in social work practice over recent decades and the effectiveness of teams in supporting service users.

## Changes over the last 40 years

Major changes in social attitudes occurring over the last 40 years have impacted on the social work task and the public view of the profession. The earlier objective as set out by Eileen Younghusband was to help a service user become 'more at ease with himself and others and have a bit more elbow room in his social circumstances'. The modern view expects more dramatic improvements both in the service users' relationships and environment, while the issues for service users remain as challenging as before and human nature as fallible as ever.

Some of the changes include:

- the move to community care and closure of large long-stay institutions;
- public wish for greater integrated care between health and social services (e.g. for older people with multiple needs);
- preference for the medical model of cure by specialists rather than understanding the impact of the emotional needs of people on their health;
- local authorities ceasing to be prime providers of social services, instead becoming customers with service provision competitively contracted out;
- tightness of local authority budgets given the pressure on government to reduce taxation – and reluctance to decentralise budgets back to localities;
- greater expectation of local accountability for both quality and cost of services, with increased risk of media criticism of local authorities and social work management;
- the growth of the blame culture as shown in the media's vilification of individual social workers involved in child tragedies;
- the increased complexity of legislation (e.g. *Grogan* judgment) and peoples' awareness of their rights and the ability to challenge through the courts;
- greater plurality of background and ethnicity;
- reduction in common culture and divergent views on the role of public support services such as social work, public health and education;

- expectation of equal treatment of men and women both in the community and staff work force, with equal opportunities for women in senior management;
- more flexible working arrangements (e.g. job shares; parents allowed to work child-friendly hours);
- prosperity and growing inequalities in wealth leading to greater intolerance of vulnerable people;
- physical ill-treatment of children is no longer tolerated and the need for child safeguarding recognised, but community preventive services have been reduced;
- more tolerant attitudes to sexuality, but more awareness of the risk of abuse.

## Are social work teams more or less effective than 40 years ago?

Modern social work teams are helping many more people than we supported in the 1970s and 1980s. Medical advances in the last 20 years have dramatically increased life spans, leading to increased demand for specialist care and support services. The District Team worked with a high number of people, aged between 19 and 64, who previously would have died from heart attacks and strokes, as well as from head and brain injuries following road traffic injuries. Most of the team's work required a brief assessment for services, but the more satisfying interventions required skilled professional judgement on complex situations.

The number of service providers is much greater – as well as the amount of legislation and underpinning audit trail. But the motivation and core values of the social workers have not changed. It was heart-warming to witness sensitive and skilled work in so many diverse areas. But, as set out below, there was a considerable variation in the quality of the support environments for the teams based on the five factors identified.

Given the complexity and increase in legislation, it is more challenging nowadays to work out how to implement policies locally. The professional skills of the social workers continue to be high, though the greater work pressures have constrained the continuous learning opportunities. Despite the risk of blame when things go wrong and limited delegation of budgets given the financial tightness, I was struck by the social workers' determination to make thoughtful professional judgements on the ground. Managers were committed and worked hard in this pressurised environment to ensure manageable work flows and maintain close contact with their teams. It was evident, however, that supervision needs to be reinvigorated to provide enough mental space for social workers to reflect effectively on situations, both of service users and themselves.

## Are team leaders and area managers as effective?

The team leaders and area managers in the three teams were strong and doing a good job. They were liked by their staff and gave them the freedom to take decisions on the ground. Compared to 40 years ago when we were inventing systems on the hoof, these managers could hold their heads high. They were coping well with the range of new legislation, the risk of media blame, and high demand from the community.

They needed more help through technology investment to handle the growing information overload and ability to communicate with social workers expecting to work more flexibly. They would also have benefited from standard modern management development tools such as 360-degree feedback (e.g. on their chairing of management meetings to ensure all participate fully). Some provided insufficient formal supervision, and relied too much on informal interactions to provide mental space. Management training was needed before promotion on how to provide supervision amid all the other pressures.

## Are new social workers better educated and trained?

The professional decision in the 1970s to deliver integrated generic qualifying courses initially put pressure on the education system. The qualifying courses[1] need large curricula in order to cover the generic skills needed for children and family legislation, for mental health legislation, and for work with people having physical disabilities and learning disabilities, dementia and problems of old age. This breadth is demanding both to teach and learn. There have been differing views on how far students should study generic issues such as 'intervening in a crisis' rather than client-specific issues such as 'troubled adolescence' or 'depression in old age'. In the field it became clear that no one could expect to be an expert at the outset of their career across the whole range of legislation and practice interventions – but that an important advantage of generic training is the spread of shared social work values across the workforce.

When the demands of the community care reforms were introduced in the 1990s, many authorities took the opportunity to reorganise into separate teams for adults and for children. There was a perceptible drop in the number of enthusiastic and dedicated recruits to social work in the late 1980s and early 1990s. To encourage quality recruitment, social work followed nursing and introduced a degree course which started in 2003. This replaced the two-year diploma in social work provided since 1991.

I have been impressed by the quality of the students I have taught on the Masters course in social work at the Tavistock Clinic. They are as dedicated as my contemporaries, and with the advantage of greater ethnic diversity for our multi-racial society. It is essential that there are employment opportunities so that social care providers and service users will benefit from this new expertise.

It was a boom time for employment when I first looked for a job after qualifying, but it is much tougher now. A number of the talented and sensitive people from a wide range of ethnic backgrounds that I have taught have had difficulties in finding initial employment. This is due to the financial constraints for local authorities, and their consequent reluctance to invest in the induction of newly qualified social workers. As a tutor, I advise my students to show they are indispensable in their final placement, increasing their chance of temporary employment that may become permanent. These able students need to be supported, hence it is important that university bursaries are not reduced (e.g. due to diversion of funding to the new fast-track postgraduate programmes, etc.).

## Are potential social workers attracted from sufficiently diverse backgrounds to relate to service users?

When I started social work in 1968, the profession mainly attracted people from a white middle-class background. Fortunately the expansion of subsidised higher education in the 1970s and 1980s, along with the Open University and part-time higher degrees, has provided opportunity for a much wider intake of people, in terms of race, social class and sexual orientation, to train as social workers as a first or second career.

Service users now also come from a broader range of cultural backgrounds in our multi-ethnic society, reflecting immigration and social change. Local authorities and higher education institutions have been effective in recruiting more diverse social work students who are better able to engage with these different service users. Potential social workers need to be empathetic, mature enough to understand their own prejudices, and have good verbal reasoning skills.

But management support on the job is crucial especially when there are cultural differences between a social worker and service user. Reports on tragedies often show how quickly provision in difficult situations can unravel. If a manager is off sick and under-functioning the support framework will be threatened, putting service users at risk.

### Are social workers getting a broad enough experience to be able to add value to integrated working between professionals?

Sometimes the teaching and medical profession can undervalue the social work role, but it is important that the professionalism of social workers is accepted on an equal footing. Strong management support for continuous learning is needed to develop imaginative interprofessional practice. For example, Kelly, a senior social worker at the hospital, was studying multi-disciplinary working for her advanced award.

There also need to be staff swaps, joint training sessions to work on case studies, agreed checklists, and other ways of understanding and developing working relationships. The area office where I set up my intake group was opposite a state-of-the-art new hospital. After some months of inappropriate referrals from the social work department, we had a joint meeting. During a two-week swap with an orthopaedic social worker, I discovered the hospital staff knew little about our process of assessment and allocation. Both the relationships and the systems improved when this was clarified.

I was reminded of this while studying the Hospital Team. Some of the medical staff took insufficient responsibility for the discharge arrangements for patients. Unless NHS staff go half way to understand the discharge procedure, these problems will continue. A friend was assured by the occupational therapist (OT) that she would be discharged home after a three-month stay. Nothing happened – the OT had failed to make a referral to the social worker. But the social worker was blamed for incompetence. There needs to be greater cooperation if the community is to benefit from a joint health and social care service. Leaders from both sides need to show the way.

### Are social workers reflecting sufficiently on service users' issues?

Service users have very different problems and needs. Their fundamental emotional needs have not changed over the years, though the numbers continue to increase. Children without a containing adult are more likely to develop borderline traits, and become parents with difficulties with their own children. Without adequate support, social workers find it difficult to withstand the negative projections from these 'hard-to-reach' service users.

The social workers in the three teams thought carefully and imaginatively about the people and their situations. Forty years ago, it was more hit and miss to catch the attention of a social worker. Opportunities for discussion with other social workers varied across the three teams. This was always part of the Mental Health Team's approach. It happened daily in the small group rooms in the hospital but in an unstructured way. When I left, the District Team staff set up a regular case discussion group so they also benefited – previously this had been a rare opportunity.

Society's ambivalence toward dependent adults and those with long-term needs makes the role of the social worker particularly challenging. To be effective, social workers need the mental space to understand users' needs and to reflect on how help can be provided. Teams perform better if they have a supportive environment, but I found in some of the teams that formal supervision was often squeezed out and not given priority due to work pressures.

### Are social workers swamped with demand?

In the 1970s social workers were under pressure of referrals. That is still the case as people are living longer, often in stressful situations. The numbers of service users will probably go on rising as society continues to expect the state rather than the family to support those in need. Hence, skills in demand management are essential. Social workers need to be able to prioritise requests to a manageable level, so they can then have the time and mental space to use their professional skills effectively in supporting service users. Children's services can easily be overwhelmed by undifferentiated referrals (e.g. if the police pass on all domestic violence incidents with no intelligent assessment of risk). The ability to handle all the work coming in to a social work office depends on clear guidelines for referrers, and knowledgeable and equable managers – as I met in all three teams.

Everyone in the District Team realised they had to keep the work flowing. This was well managed due to an expert handling the telephones, the support of experienced locums along with regular intervention by the team leaders. But the system was finely balanced and could easily become overloaded by an unexpected complaint or employment issue that demanded days of preparation. The Hospital Team handled delayed discharges speedily through a specialist discharge officer, step-down beds, and eagle-eyed monitoring by the operations manager. But there was insufficient time to meet the emotional needs of some patients. The Mental Health Team as a specialist provider was able to manage demand more easily. There could, however, be difficulties if other providers failed to cooperate (e.g. if a local hostel refused to accept a referred service user).

Overall, the effort in the three teams to prioritise referrals was laudable. This enabled more responsibility to be delegated to social workers, which would have been unrealistic if overloaded. We hear regularly of departments where social workers are working unacceptably long hours to handle their caseload with serious risk of misjudgements through fatigue. It is vital that best practice is shared across the country, for example from these three teams. We were certainly no better 40 years ago.

### Is care in the community working?

The majority of large long-stay institutions have closed. These were for the mentally ill, people with learning disabilities, or people with severe brain damage. In contrast prisons have doubled their capacity over this period from 40,000 to 80,000 inmates. Care in the community has been welcome for many service users now able to live more independent lives, but this has come at a financial and social cost. There is often considerable unease in local communities when small homes and hostels are planned in the vicinity.

A student told me that she and other young people were frightened of becoming old. This fear is exacerbated by the pressures of social media to 'be perfect' which can encourage prejudice, if not hatred, against vulnerable people in the community – in some cases leading to occasional ill-treatment or worse. The provision of a named social worker for all people with learning disabilities, autism, or chronic mental illness is important to improve safety and quality of life. But society and the government need to invest the necessary resources to implement this effectively.

### Are modern approaches to preventive mental health effective?

There have been massive changes in the approach to mental health. Forty years ago, disparaging remarks about 'loony bins' and 'nutters' were common. Having had low priority for many decades, mental health is now being recognised as a major problem for society, with one in four people having some mental health issue during their life. The emphasis is on helping people to live in the community, in smaller hostels or residential care. This comes at a cost and substantial funding will be needed in the future.

Mental health teams in the community address early onset disorders in young people as well as crisis intervention for the acutely ill. More, well-staffed local in-patient units are needed to provide a safe place for those with acute psychosis or suicidal tendencies. If patients are able to stay closer to their homes, then recovery and future treatment can be better managed.

Research into the effects of long-term conditions, whether physical or mental, has produced important results in the last two decades. Richard Layard's study of psychological therapies pointed out the need for more focus on cognitive behaviour therapy, meditation and mindfulness, along with daily physical activity.[2] This can help the body's reaction to bipolar disorder, depression, anxiety, diabetes, cardiac issues, cancer and more. There is an urgent need to introduce teenagers to the benefits of psychological therapies to give them the skills to come through the emotional roller coaster of adolescence.

The Mental Health Team demonstrated the effectiveness of a specialist group and the value of detailed professional knowledge with interdisciplinary working. So yes, modern approaches to mental health are having a welcome effect. But the scale of the challenge is greater than expected, and will need the necessary resources.

### Did the move away from local authorities as the prime provider of social services change the quality of social work provision?

On the one hand competitive tendering has brought benefit through greater choice of providers, kept on their toes. For example, there is now greater flexibility in the provision of home care services. These were once only available between 9 am and 5 pm, so home-helps could return to their school-age children. After a strike led by the union against flexible working, the in-house service in my borough was closed and staff applied for employment with new providers.

On the other hand, it is more challenging for the local authority to have sufficient expertise in commissioning quality services without the hands-on experience of providing support. There are also administrative overheads and costs. Overall the greater diversity of providers has been beneficial – including residential homes run by charities, and valuable management skills brought by some of the new private sector providers. But careful monitoring is needed to ensure quality, given the pressures to save money. Local authorities are in a weak position in negotiations, particularly for residential care for older people. Standards of care are always a serious concern. In the past social workers were probably in closer contact with local authority homes in monitoring and appraising the service.

---

**Woodside – home for seven people with severe dementia**

In the 1980s, we were able to experiment with pilots, such as smaller establishments: I spent an afternoon here sitting in the heart of the house – the kitchen – seeing how the residents occupied their time. The staff were all qualified social workers. There was no TV and no line of chairs. Instead, three attractively dressed elderly women were helping to make biscuits for tea.

A social worker was helping two men set the table, while I could see the two others and another social worker outside walking around the garden. Posters on the wall gave the address of the home, who lived there, and the weather. Five years later it was closed as uneconomic. I wish that I had taken photographs to capture the atmosphere. I am not aware of many similar establishments today.

---

### What are the implications of prosperity?

The country is more prosperous than 40 years ago. The budgets for local authorities have increased, but so have society's expectations and the number of service users. Large numbers of the wealthier people in the South East pay for private medical care and schooling, etc. and exclude themselves from the public services that the rest of us rely on. This has led to a hardness and impatience by wealthier groups in positions of power toward those who need help, which is noticeable in the views of parts of the more right-wing press.

### How have society's views changed on physical ill-treatment, neglect and emotional abuse?

The safeguarding of children is a high priority both in the health and social care services. There is agreement in general that the physical ill-treatment of children, including smacking, is not acceptable. Forty years ago, it was quite different. I asked the council's medical officer to look at a six-year-old boy's bruised thigh. The boy said that this was caused by his mother throwing a shoe at him because he would not get dressed. The doctor was quite clear as she knew the family well. She said that the child was so irritating she was not surprised the mother had thrown the shoe. That was the end of the matter as far as the doctor was concerned. The safety of children is now paramount, but still unease remains as the risk of child tragedy has not been eradicated.

### How significant are changes in public attitudes to sexuality?

Attitudes to sexuality are more complex and contradictory than those of the 'Swinging Sixties'. There is greater sensitivity to the exact age of teenage girls – and more concern on underage sexual activity and considerable awareness of potential exploitation. In the 1990s, I supervised a member of staff who was a militant lesbian. One day I found her tearful and upset. She explained that she had just learnt that the older woman who had seduced her in her teens could have been accused of 'abusing' her. The fact that she had been under 16 years of age had not previously occurred to her.

## Are we developing the next generation of social work managers?

The Social Work Reform Board began funding local authorities in 2012 to provide first-line managers with training in reflective supervision. But its implementation has not yet reached every department. Hence the new 'Firstline' management training programme is welcome, especially if encompassing the five factors highlighted in this book. Reflective supervision is most important but the other factors also need to be in place, particularly a focus on management and leadership.

Unfortunately, following the closure of the College of Social Work in 2015, leadership training for senior managers (directors of children and adult services, assistant directors, and area managers) was not taken forward. Skills for Care, the training body for adult social care, supports the National Skills Academy for Social Care, which runs useful leadership and management programmes. But it is important that these encourage learning from a wide range of professions. Aspiring social work managers need to learn alongside managers from other sectors such as the health service, charities and business.

A small cohort of medical professionals is gradually rising to become chief executives of large NHS trusts. Similarly, more directors of children and adult services with strong senior management skills should be in the recruitment pool for local authority chief executives or chief executives of hospital trusts. More senior leaders are needed to speak for the profession in the media so that social work is recognised as a crucial public service that needs to be properly resourced – as well as offering an interesting and challenging career for motivated young people and others with a variety of life experience.

## Notes

1 CQSW – Certificate of Qualification in Social Work from 1975–1991; DipSW – Diploma in Social Work 1991–2003; bachelor's and master's degree in social work from 2003.
2 Layard, R. and Clark, D. 2014. *Thrive: the power of evidence-based psychological therapies.* London: Penguin.

# 12

# WHAT NOW?

### How does your team rate?

It is now your turn to look critically at the quality of support for your teams to help them operate at the best level they are capable. Some organisations are slow in giving people chances to stretch themselves. Why not complete the exercises suggested at the end of Chapters 6 to 10? You could then talk to someone at work about the points raised here and together introduce a discussion at a management or team meeting. You and your team could then introduce appropriate changes over six months which could provide new development opportunities for members of your team. Then you can jointly complete Table A1.2 on page 132 and check the changes.

### Implications for social workers

#### *Find opportunities for continuous learning*

Social workers need to keep up to date on new developments and share best practice. This means seizing development opportunities that arise (e.g. making a presentation at a team meeting or setting up a meeting on a specific issue, etc.). The PQ award system provides a valuable target to aim toward. The induction of new staff needs to include visits to the most relevant community resources. This allows social workers to gain a sense of the community they have joined.

#### *Use management meetings*

Social workers need to speak up at management and team meetings, and make sure that any confusion on policy implementation on the ground is discussed – as well as the emotional needs of service users, particularly if there is excessive pressure to achieve through-put of numbers rather than meeting their longer term needs.

#### *Make sure that mental space for reflection is available*

When applying for a post, social workers need to establish what sort of regular mental spaces will be available – for example:

- the nature and availability of regular supervision?
- case discussion groups?
- allocation meetings?

- consultancy?
- joint working with more experienced colleagues?
- in-house training?
- relying on peers?

Social workers need to understand the team dynamics and choose to work in a culture that enhances their energy and creativity. As one social worker said, 'You must have a vision of where you are going or you will be pushed around both professionally and personally'.

## Implications for first-line managers

### *Management training*

The social work profession does not provide enough basic management training for first-line managers. It is welcome that the Office of the Chief Social Worker is addressing this by supporting a new training initiative. Most managers employed by local authorities eventually complete some in-house human resources and financial management training, sometimes continuing to a master's course in advanced social work with leadership and management modules. But voluntary providers are rarely able to access this type of training. Managers need to learn how to challenge their organisation on poor accommodation, inadequate IT, lack of financial support services – and sort out the team's work priorities with the referring agencies to avoid overload.

Training in management procedures is needed before taking up a post, followed by learning skills in clinical supervision. Managers will then be more effective in nurturing teams and pressing for resources, feeding back on policy implementation and contributing to qualitative performance indicators. These two aspects of management training need to be dovetailed into the PQ framework. The first-line manager is in a key position to encourage staff development. Managers need personal development opportunities such as short 'job-swaps' across or between organisations (e.g. other local authorities or hospitals). They are then more likely to recognise similar opportunities for their staff.

### *Good management practice*

This research shows how an already stressful work environment deteriorates without well-chaired team meetings. Performance-management systems with frank but supportive annual appraisals are essential. This allows both support and challenge for team members as appropriate, and provides encouragement rather than ineffectual sympathy.

### *Supervision and the need for mental space to reflect*

Social services managers need to ensure that front-line social workers have time to reflect on their work rather than putting excessive emphasis on the provision of information to meet management performance targets. Being busy is easier than thinking about a disturbing or frightening situation – and it is important that social workers have adequate space for reflection.

Unless managers are already practised in standing back in a third position to think about the difficult dynamics of their work, they are unlikely to be able to help their staff.

Managers are best able to develop these skills if they have become practice supervisors, have undertaken a specific course in supervision, or received good-quality supervision themselves.

## Implications for senior managers

### *Leadership in communication to the public and profession*

The three teams protected the local community from the impact of numerous distressing or alarming situations – for example, a young man with brain damage behaving violently in public, or a physically and mentally frail older person being bullied by a young relative. Given this protective screen and ignorance about their neighbours, members of the community are able to split off their primitive fears and vilify both service users and social workers.

Hence, senior social work managers and leaders of the profession need to become more skilled in media communications to influence public opinion on the value of social work. Funders and opinion formers need to understand that social work intervention is often difficult to quantify (e.g. someone gaining independence in sheltered housing for the first time in 30 years, or an adult son with alcoholism being welcomed for Christmas). These smaller vignettes need sharing.

The social services might learn from the London acute hospital that ran a popular weekly slot on its A&E services on national television for some years. The BBC has broadcast some high-quality studies of children's services[1] but has yet to develop these into an effective recruitment series such as 'Call the Midwife'. Some prejudices might also be dissipated if social work managers participated regularly at community forums and if local offices were encouraged to hold 'open days'.

### *Learning leadership and management skills*

Senior managers can enhance their leadership skills through education and training opportunities. More learning is needed of best practice in other public sector organisations including the health, education and voluntary sectors both in the UK and overseas (e.g. through short study visits).

There was a perception in this study that senior managers rarely 'walked the walk' and were seen as remote from the social work teams. This perception could be changed by regular visits to district offices, weekly bulletins to all staff, and central forums where social work staff can discuss current issues with the departmental management team. Managers need to spend more time explaining to staff the purpose of policy changes. This means talking to larger groups of staff, and meeting the teams in their working environment. This type of active leadership raises morale, and helps to ensure that coherent procedures backed up by good management practice are clearly communicated throughout the organisation.

### *Ensuring that all five factors are in place to support social work teams*

The social workers involved in recent child protection tragedies clearly lacked a supportive environment. The inquiries have highlighted the absence of leadership, weak management structures and poor administration. They have also noted the collapse of supervision and shortage of mental space for social workers grappling with shocking challenges – as well as the lack of prioritisation and demand management needed to avoid overload and consequent exhaustion. Senior managers need to ensure that all of the five factors identified in this book are addressed and properly resourced for their social work staff.

### Influencing the allocation of resources

The voice of senior social work management needs to be heard at the top table of local authorities and health trusts in discussion on budget allocations. There is a perception that social work is readily marginalised by the more powerful professional bodies in education and health. For example, in the education department, schools may receive money at the expense of children in need and child protection – while in the mental health trusts, the pharmaceutical and nursing budgets may be funded at the expense of social work support for people in mental distress. Senior social work managers need to be seen by their staff to negotiate robustly for a fair share of the centrally allocated funds, and to feed back to policy makers on the effectiveness of new policies.

Senior managers need to ensure the provision of good office environments, IT resources, and support staff for social workers. Without these support structures, social workers are unable to fulfil their role, and their confidence in senior managers is lowered. Delegation of resources to the teams enhances their commitment, autonomy and creativity. It encourages local community involvement, partnerships with smaller voluntary groups and the potential for innovative ways of working. For example, social workers would benefit by working in pairs to share expertise and understanding of difficult situations.

### Performance management

Performance management is important. But senior managers need to reappraise outcomes and success to make sure that performance indicators reflect qualitative as well as quantitative aspects. This means less prescriptive assessment forms and more focus on reflective leadership and the emotional needs of service users. Therapeutic supervision and mentoring should be provided separately from performance management. Social workers and managers need the energy and creativity found in shared mental space to work effectively with excluded and marginalised service users.

## Implications for national bodies

### National training and skills development

The General Social Care Council improved the profession's performance through registration and the PQ framework along with initial qualification at degree level. However, first-line management training needs to be included within the PQ framework. This would help best practice in clinical supervision and more widespread provision of mental space for social work teams. External bodies, including universities and the National Skills Academy in Social Care, should continue to work with employers to provide mandatory management training for social work and social care line managers before or within three months of taking up post.

## *Confusion in implementation of policies*

There can be confusion on the implementation of some policies for social workers on the ground given the complexity of the law and its interpretation – as noted earlier in relation to 'no recourse to public funds' and 'continuing care'. Following any subsequent legal judgments, government needs to provide rapid advice to community teams across the country on their interpretation. This is needed to save time and frustration locally. New policies need to be piloted and their implementation assessed before changes are made. With different approaches to implementation, services could be compared and contrasted, and best practice adopted more widely. In addition, local authorities need to involve the social workers in the preparation of guidance and procedures based on national policies to try to reduce teething problems.

## *Coherence of policies*

Over recent years, national social work bodies have fragmented and social workers have lacked a strong unified professional institution. The development and maintenance of a shared vision has become harder. The social work role itself has become more complex and interdisciplinary with other professions. For example, other professionals undertake counselling, advocacy and 'best interest assessments' – areas once the preserve of social workers.

Health and social care services are increasingly expected to work cohesively together – partly in the interest of better care for service users and partly for financial savings (e.g. reducing length of stay in hospitals). In the longer term a fully integrated health and social care model will have major implications for the organisation of social work. The split of policy between the Department of Health and Department for Education has added another complication, with adults and children being considered separately. Hence, the setting up of the Office of Chief Social Worker is a welcome step if the two Chief Social Workers can help facilitate consistency in policy formulation at the national level and guidance to local providers and social workers on the front line.

## Final comment

This is a time of great change in social work, and challenge for social workers and managers. For example:

- Social workers with adults implementing the Care Act 2014 are finding there are cuts to care packages, problems in meeting demands for an advocacy service and continuing shortages in the number of social workers.
- There is growing demand from service users. For example, the number of children being referred to children's departments for risk assessment has massively increased. Over one in five children born in 2009/10 were referred over suspected abuse.[2] This runs the risk of diverting social workers carrying out these assessments from other critical tasks – including new initiatives such as the government drive to prioritise adoption over short-term foster care placements and to provide greater support for young people leaving care.

- The Children and Social Work Bill may allow the government to directly regulate social workers. Not surprisingly, the British Association of Social Workers is concerned that professional standards will be affected by short-term political priorities rather than the profession's evidence-base.

These new demands are putting further pressure on social workers. Hence it has never been more important to look after your staff if they are to look after others. You will find that implementing the five enabling factors discussed in this book will help you to build and maintain the effective social work teams which are so needed by service users.

## Notes

1 For example, the BBC programme covering the Bristol Children's Services in 2004 – 'Someone to watch over me' and 'Protecting our children' (2012).
2 Study by Professor Andy Bilson, School of Social Work, Care and Community, University of Central Lancashire. *British Journal of Social Work*. May 2016.

# APPENDIX 1

# STRENGTH OF THE FIVE FACTORS FOR THE TEAMS

### Enabling environment needed to support social work teams

The study of the three teams shows how good support environments based on the five factors identified can help social work teams, and indicates their relative quality in underpinning effectiveness.

### *The coherence of national and local policies for the three teams*

Each of the teams had clear national guidance and the legal framework was understood by the well-trained social workers. These had been agreed by the council and disseminated to staff. Problems in interpreting the guidance for policy implementation often occupied the mental space of managers and social workers, particularly in the District and Hospital Teams, leaving less time for thinking about the actual needs of service users.

The Hospital Team had a major challenge in dealing with delayed discharge legislation. The team achieved the objective of freeing up beds. However, this led to the social workers feeling they were part of a conveyor belt with patients becoming objectified and their emotional needs not being met. There was confusion on 'continuing care policies', such as how to interpret the implications of the Grogan judgment on the ground. The Mental Health Team felt that the repressive nature of 'no recourse' legislation conflicted with their professional values.

### *Professional skills in the three teams*

The teams had well-qualified and professionally motivated staff with positive attitudes and a determination to meet service user need. But the opportunities for further development and learning varied. There was no overall plan to ensure continuous learning within the District and Hospital Teams. Many social workers in these teams had come into post determined to complete the PQ award to improve their practice and career prospects. They often had to fight hard for the opportunity as the budget had been given to the new children's service.

Social workers in the District and Hospital Teams had few development opportunities in their day-to-day work. The Hospital Team social workers had no role model to follow when attending the weekly ward meetings. This exposed new inexperienced workers to the risk of oppressive 'dumping' of discharge cases onto them.

All the social workers in the Mental Health Team had become ASWs (now approved mental health practitioners), and the CPNs were completing further professional training. They were all given different responsibilities with developmental opportunities. Much of the work in the Mental Health Team was carried out in pairs unlike that in the District and Hospital Teams. This had benefits, as the social workers and CPNs gained expertise from this joint working.

The Mental Health Team had high morale and was well motivated. Most of the staff in the District Team and the Hospital Team were also well motivated, though the latter had some disengaged staff.

### Management support structures in the three teams

All three teams had competent team leaders and clear overall objectives. They needed well-chaired and focused management meetings. In practice, the District Team's fort-nightly team meeting lacked time boundaries, participative discussion and an effective decision-making structure. The fortnightly team meeting of the Hospital Team was well managed and reasonably participative. The Mental Health Team also achieved effective discussion with their weekly team and case discussion meetings.

The District Team had good internal IT and business support, but time was wasted dealing with the changing records system. The Hospital Team had the least effective administrative and IT support. Team members spent hours typing assessment forms, and entering invoices on the IT system. The Mental Health Team's multi-disciplinary staff group was deployed flexibly, and was the only staff group who did not complain about the IT system or the demands of record keeping.

### Autonomy in the three teams

Clear objectives are essential to empower social workers so they can take decisions on the ground in a timely way for service users. But the objectives for the District and Hospital Teams did not sufficiently encompass the emotional as well as material needs of service users.

Social workers need discretion on how to best allocate their time to engage with service users to understand their needs. This is difficult if workloads are too high. The District Team managers worked hard to free up the social workers to have some dis-cretion in use of time to help service users. However, the social workers disliked the centralisation of budget spend, which meant they could no longer sign off small amounts (e.g. meals on wheels).

Despite its success in delivering its formal goals, the Hospital Team was in the diffi-cult position of handling a relentless throughput to meet targets to free up beds – with inevitable adverse impact on the team's autonomy. In contrast, the Mental Health Team had considerable autonomy, and was able to be selective on the choice of service users supported.

### The availability of mental space in the three teams

Social workers in the District Team had few formal opportunities to discuss their work. They looked for informal contact with experienced colleagues, which were their main occasions for developing practice. Supervision was patchy. Managers would meet with staff for specific reasons, but there were few regular supportive sessions. The District Team had the most disruptive accommodation, with no quiet space to work or think, and the overall noise produced considerable stress.

The multi-disciplinary ward meetings in the hospital did not allow for discussion or a sharing of perspectives. The culture was hierarchical rather than democratic, with insufficient opportunity for reflection, discussion or creative problem solving. Without supervision or effective multi-disciplinary meetings on the wards, discussion was dependent on the team meeting. This was the only wider forum in which they could explore together how to develop multi-disciplinary relationships within the hospital and across the social services department. The Hospital Team had to rely on each other for reflective discussion, particularly given the collapse of the management structure. The remaining managers formally replaced supervision with an 'open door' policy to cover the staffing crisis.

The Mental Health Team benefited from the structured opportunities for mental space along with democratic decision making, shared responsibilities, creative approaches to service users, a safe working environment and an appreciation of each other's specialist skills. Being a specialist team they were able to manage the work flow. The team had regular supervision, and put high priority on informal mental space for the team.

### Assessment of the quality of the support environments for the teams

Table A1.1 below and Figure A1.1 opposite set out the enabling factors for each of the teams. Clearly, simple numerical figures need to be treated with care and some are

*Table A1.1* Summary of the strength of the enabling factors for each team

| District (D) Team; Hospital (H) Team; Mental Health (M) Team | D Team | H Team | M Team |
|---|---|---|---|
| **Coherent policies** | **10** | **11** | **12** |
| Clear national guidance and legal framework | 4 | 4 | 4 |
| Coherent local policies agreed and disseminated | 4 | 4 | 4 |
| No confusion implementing policies on the ground | 2 | 3 | 4 |
| **Professional skills** | **9** | **8** | **12** |
| Well-qualified and experienced staff | 4 | 4 | 4 |
| Continuous learning opportunities encouraged | 2 | 2 | 4 |
| High morale and motivation | 3 | 2 | 4 |
| **Management support structures** | **8** | **8** | **11** |
| Leadership by managers | 3 | 3 | 3 |
| Adequate resources: financial, IT | 3 | 2 | 4 |
| Regular team meetings with good communication | 2 | 3 | 4 |

| | | 9 | 6 | 11 |
|---|---|---|---|---|
| Autonomy | | | | |
| | Clear agreed objectives for social workers | 3 | 4 | 4 |
| | Time to understand users without overload | 3 | 1 | 4 |
| | Discretion to plan interventions | 3 | 1 | 3 |
| Mental space | | 8 | 6 | 11 |
| | Regular supportive discussion with manager | 3 | 2 | 4 |
| | Time for reflection with colleagues | 3 | 3 | 3 |
| | Time and physical environment for creativity | 2 | 1 | 4 |
| **Total (max. 60):** | | **44** | **39** | **57** |

**30–39 satisfactory; 40–49 good; 50–60 outstanding**
Score per subheading: 1 low, 2 just satisfactory, 3 good,
   4 outstanding

arguably too low or high. Nevertheless taken in conjunction with the text, they give an overview of the relative strengths and weaknesses of the support environments in which the teams were operating.

Table A1.1 and Figure A1.1 show how the three teams scored on the five enabling factors in the research project. Why not get your team together to do an assessment now (using Table A1.2) and, if you are interested in making changes, repeat it in six months time?

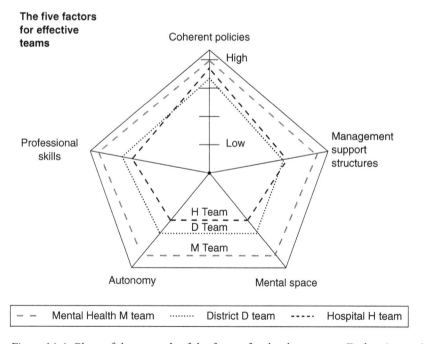

*Figure A1.1* Chart of the strength of the factors for the three teams. Each axis runs from 0 to 12. Each team is marked on the relevant axis. The dots have been joined to show the comparison of the support environments for the three teams.

*Table A1.2* How does your team rate?

| The five factors for effective social work teams | | Max. | Your team |
|---|---|---|---|
| Coherent policies | | 12 | |
| | Clear national guidance and legal framework | 4 | |
| | Local policies agreed and disseminated | 4 | |
| | No confusion implementing policies on the ground | 4 | |
| | | | |
| Professional skills | | 12 | |
| | Well-qualified and experienced staff | 4 | |
| | Continuous learning opportunities encouraged | 4 | |
| | Morale high and staff energised | 4 | |
| | | | |
| Management support structures | | 12 | |
| | Leadership by managers | 4 | |
| | Adequate resources: financial, IT | 4 | |
| | Regular team meetings with good communication | 4 | |
| | | | |
| Autonomy | | 12 | |
| | Clear agreed objectives for social workers | 4 | |
| | Time to understand users without overload | 4 | |
| | Discretion to plan interventions | 4 | |
| | | | |
| Mental space | | 12 | |
| | Supportive monthly supervision with manager | 4 | |
| | Time for daily reflection on cases with colleagues | 4 | |
| | Time and physical environment for creativity | 4 | |
| | | | |
| Total (out of 60): 30–39 satisfactory; 40–49 good; 50–60 outstanding | | 60 | |
| Score per subheading: 1 low, 2 just satisfactory, 3 good, 4 outstanding | | | |

# APPENDIX 2

# RECORD OF MEETINGS
# OF THE TEAMS

For my doctoral research in 2005/6, I wanted to compare the practice of social work teams with my own experience, and check the factors essential for the supporting environments of effective teams, particularly the availability of reflective space in which a social worker could reflect on or discuss issues. Three teams volunteered – two were in one borough and the third in another. I approached the multiple case study from an ethnographic perspective. Using my reaction to psychoanalytically informed formal observations, as well as informal participation while waiting to interview staff, I then triangulated the statements made by staff with what I observed and experienced in the work place.[1] Hence the findings are evidence-based and allow comparison with practice between the teams.

## MEETINGS OF THE DISTRICT TEAM

The people in the D Team: Andy – service manager; Annie – operations manager (maternity leave); Sonia and Leroy – team leaders; Mary – business manager; Rich and Sara (left on maternity leave) – administrative support; Tony (HIV), Hazel and Clare (maternity leave) – senior social workers; Dominic, Fiona, Jill, Kath (locum, left), Laura, Liz (locum, left), Marlene (locum), Peter (new), Sylvia (HIV), Valerie, Vivienne (returned), Yvonne, Kevin – direct payments officer.

I made 16 visits between April and July 2005, and interviewed 20 people. The following is an extract from the record of my observation on a Friday afternoon. I sat in the open-plan office, next to the duty senior from 1.45 to 5.15 pm. I made notes of everything that I observed. This extract is from the second half of this session.

### Sitting in on duty

I heard Jill ask Kevin for advice and information on the direct payments form for a duty visit she had to make. There was a general conversation about Mrs H (a destitute mother and child) competing against a radio playing in the background. They talked of a threat of judicial review. This would be based on their ordinary residence. Although being a 'no recourse' case, it did not have to be done here. Andy thought someone should ask the asylum seekers team to make some arrangements by Monday. He told Leroy that the office needed to assess the case. Leroy told me he was annoyed that the council lawyers had given in to the other borough, where Mrs H had been in a women's refuge, because these cases were a potential limitless drain on resources.

Sara answered the telephone and then asked, 'Why do they go on so on the telephone?' Leroy replied, 'To get rid of their anxieties on to you!' Andy walked over to confirm that Tony had agreed to assess the case. 'So if the senior lawyer rings, tell him that it is seven days accommodation with no prejudice and categorised as domestic violence and no recourse.' Leroy told me that the assessment was to consider Mrs H's long-term future. Liz, a bystander, argued 'She doesn't have to come back to a violent environment'. Leroy repeated, 'We have to assess'.

Rich then answered the telephone, and there was real pleasure in his voice when he said, 'I'm afraid you need the over 65s team'. Andy and Leroy had a short discussion about booking in a review and the need for formal decisions on the cases left by the HIV social worker. Andy and Sara continued to sort out the cupboard. 'Where are the books we bought for our library?' he asked. Tony was sitting in the chair and talking to Leroy about the action plan for Mrs H. He would tell the other borough that we would take on the case and would do the assessment on Tuesday.

Leroy continued with his paperwork and said that I had missed a feisty exchange with the hospital discharge people two days ago. A care package had not been logged onto the system. As this office only paid registered invoices, payment had been refused. Both the hospital and emergency duty teams occasionally forgot to record care packages on the computer system. This particularly annoyed the team.

Tony called over that he had found a self-contained studio nearby for seven days from Monday for Mrs H and her child. He asked Leroy to tell the legal department. Liz brought some case papers to Andy and asked for a copy of the letter that was used in lieu of the care plan in residential nursing care. Sara said, 'I wish someone would do a list of all the letters we are now meant to use'. Liz said Anna would know. Andy interjected, 'No. Don't ask her. She is under too much pressure – ask Dennis'.

Sara's mum rang to tell her that people were viewing her house at 9am the next morning. Leroy told me that it was bad case law, like the 'no recourse' cases, that fed the judicial review system. Meanwhile the council's legal group advised them it was cheaper to give in and provide accommodation since each challenge risked costs to the council of thousands of pounds. This meant that solicitors regularly bullied them to agree to their clients' demands by immediately threatening them with judicial review.

Leroy then remarked that while there were many good things in the system there were greedy people who manipulated it. He called Liz over to tell me about a case in point. She described a council employee who had taken long-term sick leave during which time she got a first-class degree, a husband and a baby. She was now demanding to be rehoused with 24-hour care.

## A reflective commentary

Staff had initially found the government's direct payments policy difficult to implement. The take-up had increased by 50 per cent following the appointment of a specialist officer, who was initially seen as peripheral to the team. The complexity of 'no recourse' policy was further discussed, absorbing more energy and time. The judicial review system was being misused by some solicitors to hold public bodies to ransom. This could not easily be changed. Leroy felt that they were being ridiculed by legal practitioners.

When Leroy explained the telephone transactions to Sara saying, 'They are getting rid of their anxieties on to you', he described the team's broader function in the locality. It was a good example of 'teaching on the job' when experienced staff demonstrate good practice and act as a role model to others.

Age provided the team's only simple boundary around service provision, hence Rich's delight at a referral of a person aged over 65. Rationing via the eligibility criteria took longer as it demanded assessment and judgement. Given the team's reluctance to recognise that the operations manager Annie had left for an undefined period of maternity leave, I was impressed to see the two managers tackle the caseload of a social worker who had recently left after prolonged sick leave. The mislaid books seemed symbolic of the ease with which expertise and potency in the team could be mislaid.

Leroy seemed pleased to have caught the Hospital Team's failure to log an invoice. Perhaps it counteracted his fear of being part of an 'anything else team'.

There was no single individual in the team who kept in mind the numerous different forms that had to be completed at different stages of the care management process. It meant that everyone was uncertain of one procedure or another. It never occurred to Sara, the administrative assistant, that she might start to sort it out. Hence, Liz had to telephone different people (Anna or Dennis) at other offices to find an answer. This undermined the ability of staff to carry out tasks promptly, leaving an increased number of tasks to be remembered later and increasing mental strain.

Sara's imminent departure and her plans for selling the house were intruding on the group, as was her pregnancy. Leroy explained the recent unsatisfactory history of the council's 'no recourse' work and inability to challenge rogue solicitors – another loss of potency.

I think that Leroy asked Liz to tell me about an extreme case of fraud as they were finding it difficult to manage their feelings of outrage. Not only did they suspect the service user (a former employee) of exploiting the system, but she had taken a complaint out against them when challenged. It was interesting that one of the gains of the 'sick leave' had been to have a baby.

## MEETINGS OF THE HOSPITAL TEAM

The people in H Team: Mary – service manager; Terry – operations manager; Muriel and Liz (locum) – team leaders; Kelly and Y – senior social workers; Linda, Gail, Mike, Sam and six other social workers; discharge officer, housing resettlement officer; Nick – temporary administrative assistant plus three others.

I made 14 visits which included a team meeting, a hospital 'bed meeting', a period in the office, a continuing care panel, and three MDT meetings. Three visits were in September 2005, and the rest in January and February 2006. I interviewed six members of staff: a social worker, the discharge officer, a senior social worker, the service manager, the principal officer and the operations manager. The following is an extract from the record of my observation of an MDT meeting.

### On the way to an MDT meeting

Linda mentioned the difficulty of discharging people when they still felt anxious and unwell. But there was no discretion under the new discharge policies. Linda let me come with her to the MDT meeting. On the ward we walked down the middle with about nine beds on either side. She explained that she had also been an in-patient here and remarked what a surprise that had been. She introduced me to the senior nurse, Ella. They commented on the lack of staff around that week. Then we took two chairs and squeezed into Ella's minute office.

| | |
|---|---|
| *Nurse (N)*: | Okay, we have a guy in Bed 1. He's Mr D – he's 36 years old. He's been vomiting blood. He is Somalian. We're trying to get his niece to interpret. Next is John R. He is 47 years old and has a compromised immune system. So we are barrier nursing. He is for 'resusc'. |
| | Then there is Janet V. We don't need any social input. She lives with her son. She can do her own cooking and cleaning. |
| | In bed 4 is Mr C. He is 42 years old. He has pneumonia with respiratory failure and sleep apnoea. He is the guy you saw on the right. |
| *Social Worker (SW)*: | Is there anything you can do with his sleep problem? Is it a consequence of his obesity? |
| *N*: | It's also because he has COPD (chronic obstructive pulmonary disease) as well. His sister came in and helped to wash him. Since then he has been doing it himself. He has been managing. |
| *SW*: | Do you know how he manages with things like cooking, shopping, laundry and house work? |
| *N*: | No. I think his sister is doing that for him. |
| *SW*: | So there will be no social input. |
| *N*: | In bed 5 is Mr M. He is deaf. He is 81 years old. He has an infection and epilepsy. He has dementia, hypertension and Alzheimer's. He is very restless. He physically abused the staff and was kicking at them. He probably had some type of services in place given his age. |
| *SW*: | But it depends on how he was coping before. If he was able to do things himself, he might not have been offered a service. Is he mobile? |
| *N*: | Not really. He tried to get out of bed last night and he fell. No relatives came with him. None have come to see him since he's been here. |
| *SW*: | Are they talking about a placement for him? |
| *N*: | He lives nearby. |
| | This next person has an ulcer and pyrexia. He has a bypass and chronic anaemia. He is an amputee. His amputation is on the right. He is not diabetic. He has been to a panel. And he is going to residential anyway. He is basically sorted out. |
| | The next person is Mr F. . . . |
| | Then there's Mr B. . . . |
| | In Bed 9 is Mr A. He came in with chest pains – a pulmonary oedema. He has had hypertension and raised cholesterol in the past. They are keeping him in because his relatives are due to come in and sign a form but they have not been here since he arrived. The doctor said that he would be transferred to a step-down bed. |
| *SW*: | That doesn't make sense to me. Who is his social worker? Is he talking about me or does he have another one? I don't really know anything |

|     | about Mr A. Somebody might be working with him. It looks as if he has a district social worker. |
| --- | --- |
| N: | Yes, the district social worker has been in touch. |
|     | This next man is MRSA positive. He has dressing to the wound in his right leg. He's 92. They have panel agreement for a nursing home. Can you give me a date for him to go? |
| SW: | No, I know about him but I didn't deal with him. But I can find out for you. I will let you know. I think Gail might know. |

## A summary of the reflective commentary

The arrangement of discharges sounded a challenge in the face of someone's anxiety or continued feelings of ill health and vulnerability. The central conundrum surrounding the funding of 'continuing care' was to decide where curing stopped and caring started.

Linda seemed to have an easy working relationship with the other staff and the senior nurse Ella, which I found reassuring. They appeared to have worked together for some time. They knew what to expect from each other's roles.

The important role that relatives played emerged early in the meeting. Staff appeared to rely on them to put their patients into context: for example, the Somali niece to interpret, Janet lived with her son, a sister helped her overweight brother. However, the confused and unhappy Mr M appeared to have no relatives to visit him, while Mr A could not move until his elusive relatives appeared.

I felt sorry for Mr M. who was mentioned rather brusquely. Was this due to his behaviour or to his lack of family, and therefore the absence of any sense of the person behind the illness? I wondered if his aggressive behaviour was due to the infection, as I knew was sometimes the case. I also wondered if the staff had had any training in working with people with dementia. I felt sympathy with anyone who wanted to kick against a total institution.

## The Grogan judgment and the continuing care panel

I had arranged to attend the continuing care panel chaired by Dawn, the principal officer, on Monday afternoon. The reorganisation was clearly taking its toll on the senior management team as the trade union had advised staff not to cooperate. While we waited for the meeting, she explained that she had no administrative support and had to cover for two colleagues while they attended an Industrial Tribunal.

On top of these demands, a legal judgment had just been delivered on the 'Grogan Case' (*Grogan* v *Bexley 2006*), which would affect all decisions on the funding of continuing care placements. Maureen Grogan's family had challenged the local primary care trust's decision to deny her funded care. She was chronically ill and sold her house to pay for care. The judge said that the criteria used by the NHS in their care decision had been flawed, and that Maureen Grogan should not have had to pay. The implications for the department were not known, nor for the meeting that we were about to attend. Dawn had drafted a paper for the senior management team and was seeking views of colleagues. She complained several times of a 'crisis of capacity' in the organisation. She explained that the time of the policy officer was dedicated to managing the Department of Health's performance assessment framework.

I wondered if it was a 'crisis of capacity' for the senior management team. In apparent answer to my thoughts she suddenly remarked, 'I think more desk work is needed. They say we ought to get out but I think social workers should do more at their desks'. Perhaps this sudden wish to make people sit at desks implied that they would then think hard. Was it a cry for more mental space for the organisation and the people working in it to think, reflect and digest such issues as the Grogan judgment?

At the continuing care panel I was struck by the sensitivity with which they heard and commented on the cases at the meeting. This appeared in marked contrast to the way patients were discussed on the wards. As the budget holder for the primary care trust was not present to challenge their decisions, the others may have been enjoying a break from the usual pressure and conflict.

## MEETINGS OF THE MENTAL HEALTH TEAM

The people in M Team: Dave (ASW) and Sally (CPN) – the job-share managers; Ed – psychiatrist full time; SHO (Senior House Officer); psychiatrist two sessions; consultant psychiatrist – two sessions (timed for their meetings); Wendy and Peter (CPNs full time); Lynne, Jane, Carol and Tess (CPNs part time); Julia – OT full time; Gill, Fraser, Anna – full-time ASWs; Lou – nursing student; Nancy – information officer; Hilary and Bea – administrators.

I made 14 visits over a six-week period in April and May 2006, and interviewed 11 people.

### A surface view of the Mental Health Team

The consultant psychiatrist described the service users as having 'very limited and empty lives' but they could also be volatile and occasionally violent. 'He has a long history of very aggressive and verbally abusive behaviour but I have been quite lucky and have not been screamed at or had things thrown at me.' 'She has thoughts of stabbing people, she's an alcoholic and verbally aggressive.' (These were quotes from interviews.)

### Sitting in on duty

The following is an extract from my record of an observation.

Peter was talking on the telephone about a diabetic client. He explained that the client was now physically well and had not taken anti-diabetic drugs for a year. Gill came back from her interview with Belle. Lou stood by Peter's desk waiting for him. She seemed restless, with nothing to do. Gill rang to find the whereabouts of the interpreter. The smartly dressed woman (who turned out to be the SHO and a psychiatrist and came in two half days a week) returned to join Gill. They planned to interview Belle jointly.

The SHO and Gill discussed Belle's drugs and medication. Gill said that as she was in a stable placement Belle wanted . . . (Dave and Peter left for supervision) . . . plenty of money to top up her mobile. Belle was getting support from Médecins Sans Frontières and also from a church some distance away. (Lou began to peel an orange.) They agreed to look at practical issues in this interview. When those had been addressed, they could discuss the future. Would it be a life sentence in 'bed & breakfast' accommodation? Or would she get asylum for her trauma? The SHO hoped that she would.

Gill agreed to focus on the social side. She tried to locate some food vouchers, and learnt that their provision was being discussed at a meeting the next day. She had been impressed that Belle had arrived for her appointment on time. They would do a community care assessment. Gill went to explain to Belle that they were waiting for the interpreter.

Fraser returned and talked to someone on the telephone from Street Services. He and Ed had seen the person they were talking about the previous day. He was a wanderer and slept in different places. They had drunk coffee with him at 10 am. He had been clearheaded and making sense (not yet drinking) so they had access to his mental state. This was the fourth time they had seen him. There had been no evidence of mental illness on any occasion. He said he would get back to her.

I asked Fraser about his 6 am outreach visit with Wendy. He said they had been looking for the 'silver trolley lady' but could not find her. They had seen Julie but she had just said 'Go away'. There had been no sign of the other two they had hoped to see. So they had breakfast at 8 am before coming into the office. It had been lovely at that time of day – even the railway station looked fresh and rosy.

Lou came back. Jane was repeatedly walking in and out and rather restless. She persuaded Lou to eat her lunch in the kitchen. Dave came in and offered to get lunch for Hilary. He rearranged the supervision time with Fraser. Dave went to the downstairs office, where Jane and Lynne sat, to tell them there were no clinicians upstairs, only Hilary and me. Lynne walked in with an enormous pile of files saying that she would start duty as Gill was running late. Dave came back with sandwiches for most of the office. Everyone took some time off, mainly looking up information on the web. Lynne helped Dave to translate different sailing boat accessories from German into English.

Jane came in to check with Dave about the arrangements for Leila's assessment. They talked again. Dave appeared to be reassuring her that there would be no final decision about using the Mental Health Act if Leila agreed to admission. There was also the hostel place to offer. Dave reiterated, 'There's no pressure so it shouldn't be too difficult . . .'. I thought he was reassuring himself.

Lynne answered the phone to someone who said he was a solicitor. He urgently wanted a letter from the team to support bail for a client. She remembered there was media interest in this client last time. She and Dave found a letter on the file from the previous Thursday. Dave said he was not going to be bounced into replying in 20 minutes – it just wasn't on. He suggested she told the caller that none of the people working with the client were in the office at the moment. But if we could confirm that the caller was genuine, we could fax the letter.

## A reflective commentary

Peter was acting as advocate for a diabetic client. The team were required to do a considerable amount of advocacy as other agencies had concerns about their service user group. Lou stood beside him, waiting for something to do.

The SHO and Gill worked out their different roles in the planned interview. While Belle's experiences might have induced PTSD in some people, none of the professionals could predict what the Immigration Office would decide. This meant that their planning had to be as short-term as the clients. I was conscious that this was the first team in which I had seen staff coming and going to supervision.

I was surprised when I heard the high priority Belle put on her need for money for her mobile telephone. I reflected that mobile technology had changed expectations on the ease and frequency of social contact right across the globe. The need to have an interpreter to help conduct Belle's interview demonstrated the demands and complexity of conducting assessments for non-English speakers from around the world.

When Fraser discussed a client with a colleague, I was struck by the effort they had made to be alongside the client in a way that he could tolerate. This resulted in a thorough assessment of his mental state – more than that given to many more orthodox patients.

Fraser gave me a vivid description of his outreach work that morning– the difficulty in finding people, their namelessness, the single 'Go away!' Then he described his sense of a city washed clean by the dawn, which seemed to stand in contrast to their intractable client group.

Lou returned far earlier than expected. We were all relieved when Jane persuaded her to eat her sandwich downstairs in the meeting room. Dave saw it as his responsibility to make sure everyone was sustained. As a manager, he may have felt it was part of his contribution to a good working environment similar to his interjections on non-work issues. As Hilary was answering the telephones (her colleague Bea must have been off for the day) he added her sandwich to his list.

Dave also took responsibility for the health and safety of staff. He had explained to me that their policy was to try to have two clinicians in the building at all times. As Gill was still interviewing, he asked Lynne to come to the office. When Dave returned with lunch, people took ten minutes out of the day to read or search the web for personal information unrelated to their work.

Jane at last had managed to track Dave down and to ask about his plans for Leila. Wendy had not yet come in to the office. He reassured her, but clouded the issue by mentioning the fall-back possibility of a hostel place. Dave's offer of multiple and contradictory solutions possibly reflected his own uncertainty on the best course of action or conflicting views between team members. I could not quite place Jane's anxiety and involvement as Leila was Wendy's client.

When Gill sent Belle off to one of the lunch clubs available, I was again surprised at the network of resources available to homeless people on the streets. Lynne had to deal with a suspicious telephone call. Fortunately, she remembered that the press had been involved before. She handled it cautiously and asked Dave's advice. I admired the way that they resisted acting too quickly but responded thoughtfully and with care. This corporate memory was a central component of the team's ability to provide a service for their service users.

## Being excluded and an outcast – Leila's story

The Mental Health Team brought Leila to my attention in several ways. Her situation had been discussed at my initial visit when I recorded the following notes:

> Ed described Leila as having chronic long-term psychiatric problems but she was always very pleasant and undemanding. She came up from the coast and has been rough sleeping for the last six months. While there may have been hospital admissions in the past, she was last seen by a locum psychiatrist who said there was not enough evidence to admit her. Leila presents well but must now be quite ill. She is being referred for a Mental Health Assessment now which needs to take a long-term view.

There followed a very full discussion with all eight members of the group participating. Dave asked what we would hope to achieve by admission. Was there a risk of her running off? Ed thought so. Dave thought we should be straight with her and 'share our concerns'. Ed said, 'She'd scoot! We could easily be the latest mental health professionals to be evaded'. Gill described how Leila greeted them with a kiss – Ed said he felt like 'a real Judas'.

It was evident that Dave's question 'what do we hope to achieve by admission?' was never answered. By following it with a query on the client's evasiveness, Ed had an opening to emphasise their need to be persistent. However, completing an assessment in such circumstances could quickly become persecutory. The dilemma and pain for the professionals in continuing to act in the client's interests is vividly captured by Ed's description of feeling 'a real Judas' when the unsuspecting client kissed him.

When Leila's key worker, Wendy, returned from holiday the assessment became a priority. But Jane, who had also been away at that first meeting, appeared ill at ease with the proposal, as shown in the observation above. I was unclear why.

Two weeks later I was in the office to interview Ed and then Dave. Apparently Leila's planned assessment had not taken place as another was arranged for that afternoon. I noted a sense of foreboding in the air. When invited to talk about 'a difficult situation'. Ed brought up Leila:

> Wendy and I've been concerned about her for a long time. And I feel every time we discuss it, it becomes a bit clearer in my mind because of our discussion. I have talked it through with a number of people because that helps to clarify things a bit. Hopefully it will be resolved one way or another shortly – or maybe not. For this situation we would try to get a female psychiatrist. We think that's more appropriate.

Ed did not really explain why he and Wendy had become so worried about Leila. They usually worked carefully to fit in with the longer time span often needed by homeless people. Perhaps she came over as different from the other rough sleepers with whom she associated? Perhaps she seemed older or more middle class? I was relieved that they wanted to find a woman psychiatrist for a second opinion.

Dave was also worried and perplexed at the situation, particularly its impact on relationships in the team: 'There is an assessment which has been rumbling on and might be happening this afternoon. There are a lot of complicated issues within it and potential for conflict within the team and outside the team in terms of relationships, in terms of how decisions are made.' One person said in the team meeting, 'Are you aware that I am feeling like this about it? There is a slight sort of trickiness there. It is a slightly no-win situation'.

Dave commented:

> I am aware there is a danger in a team like this which has a shared ethos and low turnover and has very good informal systems and a lot of friendship between individual team members. I think that all those things are healthy. But I think that probably if someone is coming into the team they might be struck that it might be slightly excluding at some levels. That is slightly happening here. I don't think there is a neat solution to that.

Dave was clearly concerned as to how the group would respond to this challenge. I was glad that he mentioned the disadvantages of close-knit teams for newcomers. I noted he had not yet discussed his concerns with the unnamed team member. I thought he was referring to Jane. Perhaps that was why Jane was supportive toward me, realising I was another outsider.

I was in the office the next day to interview Fraser and Nancy. Jane was on duty and asked Dave what had happened the previous day on Leila's assessment. Did it go ahead? Dave explained that the ASW had agreed she needed treatment for a psychotic illness. Jane was surprised. The psychiatrist and Wendy were both trying to obtain her agreement to go into a hostel rather than to be admitted. Leila had even said to Wendy, 'You're more upset than me'. Dave said that they had never planned to do an admission then, and had not wanted the trauma of the police and ambulance. That could be handled later. Jane attended to telephone calls and paper work, muttering in consequence of one – 'This is a horrible situation!'

The following day I interviewed Jane. As the only black clinician in the team, I had wanted to affirm her work. I asked her if she could tell me about something recent that had been quite difficult. She replied:

> Well, I have just come out of something that is quite tricky. There is a lady – a black lady in her middle age. She has been rough sleeping for some while. People have been quite concerned about her. To cut a long story short, I met her at the day centre and said to my colleague that on the face of it she does not seem acutely unwell, but she is acting in a way that is unusual for a woman and lady of her age in her mid-fifties.
>
> After a few weeks it was decided to do a Mental Health Act assessment to get her assessed. That happened yesterday. All along I was saying 'What will we do if we do section her?' A lot of black people, rather than being informally admitted or offered a different type of treatment, are sectioned and it is often their first contact with the mental health services.
>
> I am really worried because I have been involved in this work for years and years and I know what happens to black people when they do go into hospital. This lady has never been in hospital before. Why are we doing it with this one? I am not happy about it. But I don't really want to rock the boat. I feel very visible anyhow because as you can see I'm the only black clinician in the team. I do not want to alienate myself from my colleagues.

Jane was the first person to mention that Leila was black. I wondered why, and concluded that it must be a policy not to include racial background in descriptions of cases. It was also noticeable that while Ed had mentioned the benefit of using a woman psychiatrist, no one suggested using a black clinician as key worker.

### Note

1 The research technique is set out in Foster, J. 2016. 'Ethnography on the front line, why some teams struggle and others thrive'. In: G. Ruch and I. Julkunen (eds), *Relationship-based research in social work: understanding practice research*. London: Jessica Kingsley Publisher.

# REFERENCES

Adlam, J. and Scanlon, C. 2005. 'Personality disorder and homelessness: membership and "unhoused minds" in forensic settings'. *Group Analysis* 38(3): 452–466.

Ainsworth, M. 1977. 'Social development in the first year of life: maternal influences on infant-mother attachment'. In: J. Tanner (ed.), *Developments in psychiatric research*. London: Hodder & Stoughton.

American Psychiatric Association. 1987. *Diagnostic and statistical manual for mental disorders*. 3rd edn. Washington, DC: American Psychiatric Press.

Ariès, P. 1976. *Western attitudes toward death: from the Middle Ages to the present*. Baltimore, MD: Johns Hopkins University Press.

Balloch, S., Andrew, T., Ginn, J., McLean, J., Pahl, J. and Williams, J. 1995. *Working in the social services*. London: National Institute of Social Work.

Barker, M. 1982. 'Through experience towards theory: a psychodynamic contribution to social work education'. *Issues in Social Work Education* 2(1): 3–25.

Bion, W. 1962. *Learning from experience*. London: Karnac.

Borrill, C., Carletta, J., Carter, A., Dawson, J., Garrod, S., Rees *et al.* 2000. *The effectiveness of health care teams in the National Health Service*. Aston University.

Bostock, L., Bairstow, S., Fish, S. and Macleod, F. 2004. *Managing risk within child welfare: promoting safety management and reflective decision-making*. London: Social Care Institute for Excellence.

Bowlby, J. 1953. *Child care and the growth of love*. London: Penguin Books.

Bowlby, J. 1979. *The making and breaking of affectional bonds*. London: Tavistock.

Britton, R. 1989. 'The missing link: parental sexuality in the Oedipus complex'. In: Britton, R., Feldman, M. and O'Shaughnessy, E., *The Oedipus complex today: clinical implications*. London: Karnac.

Cabinet Office. 2007. 'Reaching out: think family'. London: Social Exclusion Unit.

Community Care (Delayed Discharges) Act. 2003. London: The Stationery Office.

Cooper, A. 2005. 'Surface and depth in the Victoria Climbié Inquiry Report'. *Child and Family Social Work* 10: 1–9.

Dartington, A. 1994. 'Where angels fear to tread: idealism, despondency and inhibition of thought in hospital nursing'. In: A. Obholzer and V.Z. Roberts (eds), *The unconscious at work*. London: Routledge.

Dean, M. 2012. *Democracy under attack*. London: Policy Press.

Department for Education. November 2015. 'Knowledge and skills statements for practice leaders and practice supervisors'.

Department of Health and Social Security. 1974. *Report of the committee of inquiry into the care and supervision provided in relation to Maria Colwell*. London: HMSO.

Department of Health and Home Office. 2003. *The Victoria Climbié inquiry: report of an inquiry by Lord Laming*. CM 5730. London: The Stationery Office.

Department of Health. 2003. *Fair access to care services: guidance on eligibility criteria for adult social care.* London: The Stationery Office.

Department of Health. 2003. *Direct payments guidance: community care, services for carers and children's services (direct payments) guidance England 2003.* London: The Stationery Office.

Department of Health. 2014. Care Act.

Department of Health. March 2015. 'Knowledge and skills statement for social workers in adult services'.

Department of Health. January 2016. 'Social work for better mental health'. A strategic statement. Dr Ruth Allen, Dr Sarah Carr, Dr Karen Linde with Hari Sewell.

Department of Health. 2016. 'Annual Report by the Chief Social Worker for Adults 2015–16'.

Fleming, R. 1998. 'The inner impact of work with disturbance'. In: R. Davies (ed.), *Stress in social work.* London: Jessica Kingsley.

Fonagy, P. 1991. 'Thinking about thinking: some clinical and theoretical considerations in the treatment of a borderline patient'. *International Journal of Psychoanalysis* 72: 639–665.

Foster, J. 2016. 'Ethnography on the front line, why some teams struggle and others thrive'. In: G. Ruch and I. Julkunen (eds), *Relationship-based research in social work: understanding practice research.* London: Jessica Kingsley.

Foster, J. 'Thinking on the front line – why some social work teams struggle and others thrive'. Thesis for Doctorate in Social Work awarded by the University of East London in collaboration with the Tavistock and Portman NHS Foundation Trust. http://drjudyfoster.blogspot.co.uk

Freud, S. 1920. 'Beyond the pleasure principle'. In: *The standard edition of the complete psychological works of Sigmund Freud.* Vol. XVIII. London: Hogarth Press, 1955, pp. 3–64.

Freud, S. 1922. *Group psychology and the analysis of the ego.* London: Hogarth Press and Institute of Psycho-analysis.

Garland, C. 1991. 'External disasters and the internal world: an approach to psychotherapeutic understanding of survivors'. In: J. Holmes (ed.), *Textbook of psychotherapy in psychiatric practice.* UK: Churchill Livingstone Longmans.

Gawande, A. 2010. *The checklist manifesto: how to get things right.* London: Profile Books. and tasks for the 21st Century.

Gilbert, P. 2003. *The value of everything.* Lyme Regis: Russell House Publishing.

Gilligan, J. 1996. *Violence: reflections on our deadliest epidemic.* London: Jessica Kingsley.

Gladwell, M. 2008. *Outliers: the story of success.* New York: Little, Brown.

*Grogan R. v Bexley NHS Care Trust* (2006) Neural citation number: [2006] EWHC 44 (Admin). www.bailii.org/ew/cases/EWHC/Admin/2006/44.html

Health Service Ombudsman. 2003. *NHS funding for long term care of older and disabled people.* HC 399 2nd Report. Session 2002–2003. The Stationery Office.

Healy, K. 1999. 'Clinical audit and conflict'. In: R. Davenhill and M. Patrick (eds), *Rethinking clinical audit.* London: Routledge.

HMSO. 1963. The Children and Young Person's Act 1963. London.

HMSO. 1968. *Report of the Committee on Local Authority and Allied Personal Social Services (The 'Seebohm Report').* London.

HMSO. 1989. The Children Act CMND2144.

HMSO. 1983. The Mental Health (Amendment) Act 1983. London.

HMSO. 1990. The National Health Service and Community Care Act. London.

Hoggett, P. 2000. *Emotional life and the politics of welfare.* London: Macmillan.

Kantor, J. (ed.) 2004. *Face to face with children.* London: Karnac.

Knowles, M. 1973. *The adult learner: a neglected species.* 2nd edn. Houston, TX: Gulf.

Lawlor, D. 2013. 'A transformation programme for children's social care managers'. *Journal of Social Work Practice* 27(2): 177–189.

Layard, R. and Clark, D. 2014. *Thrive: the power of evidence-based psychological therapies.* London: Penguin.

Lipsky, M. 1980. *Street level bureaucracy: dilemmas of the individual in public spaces*. New York: Russell Sage Foundation.

MacDonald, G. and Sheldon, B. 1997. 'Community care services for the mental ill: consumers' views'. *International Journal of Social Psychiatry* 43(1): 35–55.

Mattinson, J. 1992. *The reflective process in casework supervision*. 2nd edn. London: Tavistock Institute.

Mattinson, J. and Sinclair, I. 1979. *Mate and stalemate*. London: Institute of Marital Studies.

Mencap. 2001. No ordinary life. www.mencap.org.uk

Menzies, I. 1970. *The functioning of social systems as a defence against anxiety*. London: Tavistock Institute of Human Relations

Mid-Staffordshire NHS Foundation Trust Public Inquiry. Chaired by Robert Francis QC. Final report published February 2013.

Miller, E.J. and Gwynne, G.V. 1972. *A life apart: a pilot study of residential institutions for the physically handicapped and the young chronic sick*. London: Tavistock.

Moriarty, J. and Manthorpe, J. March 2016. 'The effectiveness of social work with adults'. Social Care Workforce Research Unit, King's College London.

Munro, E., 2002. *Effective child protection*. London: Sage.

Munro, E., 2011. *Munro review of child protection – final report*. Department of Education.

NRPF Network. March 2008. 'Victims of domestic violence with no recourse to public funds'. www.nrpfnetwork.org.uk/policy/Documents/nrpf_victims_dv_nrpf.pdf

NRPF Network. March 2011. 'Social services support to people with no recourse to public funds: a national picture'. www.nrpfnetwork.org.uk/policy/Documents/NRPF_national_picture_final.pdf

Obholzer, A. and Roberts, V.Z. (eds). 1994. *The unconscious at work*. London: Routledge.

Ogden, T. 1982. *Projective identification and psychotherapeutic technique*. New York: Jason Aronson.

Reivich, K. and Shatte, A. 2002. *The resilience factor*. New York: Broadway Books.

Rice, A.K. 1969. 'Individual, group and intergroup processes'. *Human Relations* 22(6): 565–584.

Rosen, G., Bairstow, S. and Marsh, P. 2003. 'Learning organisations'. Project report available from the Social Care Institute for Excellence. London.

Royal Commission on Long Term Care. 1999. *The Sutherland Report*. London: The Stationery Office.

Ruch, G. 2007. 'Reflective practice in contemporary child-care social work: the role of containment'. *British Journal of Social Work* 37: 659–680.

Ruch, G., Turney, D. and Ward, A. 2010. *Relationship based social work*. London. Jessica Kingsley.

Rustin, M. 2005. 'Conceptual analysis of critical moments in Victoria Climbié's life'. *Child and Family Social Work* 10: 11–19.

Salzberger-Wittenberg, E., Henry, G. and Osborne, E. 1985. *The emotional experience of learning and teaching*. London: Routledge.

Schneider, J.A. 2005. 'Experiences in K and –K'. *International Journal of Psychoanalysis* 86: 825–839.

Skills for Care. November 2013. *Violence against social care and support staff*. Published by Skills for Care.

Social Work Task Force. 2009. 'Building a safe, confident future'. The final report of the Social Work Task Force.

Steiner, J. 1985. 'Turning a blind eye: the cover up for Oedipus'. *International Review of Psychoanalysis* 12: 161–172.

Stevenson, O. 1998. 'It was more difficult than we thought'. *Children and Family Social Work* 3: 158–161.

Tew, J. (ed.). 2004. *Social perspectives in mental health: developing social models to understand and work with mental distress*. London: Jessica Kingsley.

Waddell, M. 1989. *Living in two worlds: psychodynamic theory and social work practice*. Free Associations.

Wheeler, W. 1999. *A new modernity?* London: Lawrence and Wishart.

Winnicott, C. 1968. 'Communicating with children'. In: R. Tod (ed.), *Disturbed children*. London: Longmans.

Winnicott, D. 1947. 'Hate in the counter-transference'. *International Journal of Psychoanalysis* 30.

Winnicott, D. 1965. 'The mentally ill on your caseload'. In: Winnicott, D. *The maturational processes and the facilitating environment*. London: Karnac.

Winnicott, D. 1965. *The maturational processes and the facilitating environment*. London: Karnac.

Winnicott, D. 1971. *Playing and reality*. Harmondsworth, Middlesex: Penguin.

Younghusband, E. 1974. 'Foreword'. In: F. Turner (ed.) *Social work treatment: interlocking theoretical approaches*. New York: Free Press.

# INDEX

abuse 22, 115, 120, 126; by carers 28; child
    protection tragedies 10; District Team 48,
    50; people with learning disabilities 22;
    vulnerability of service users 19
accountability 103, 114
administration 86, 89–90, 91, 92, 95, 109
alcohol abuse 1, 49, 57, 60
Alzheimer's 17
Ariès, Philippe 55
assessment 15, 19, 36; children 126;
    continuing care 74–75; District Team
    47, 49, 50; Hospital Team 53–54, 56, 97;
    Mental Health Team 64, 140, 141–142
asylum seekers 72, 73
attachment 23; to social worker 37
attrition 54
auditing 7
autism 12, 119
autonomy 65, 67–69, 94–101, 125, 129,
    131–132

'Baby P' (Peter Connelly) 10, 44
Barker, Mary 40–41
Bion, Wilfred 24, 27
black and minority ethnic (BME) patients
    62–63
blame culture 11, 60, 114
blind eye, turning a 43–44, 45
borderline personality disorders 1, 20–21, 33,
    117; District Team 48; Mental Health Team
    57, 59, 63
Bostock, Lisa 42–43, 103
boundaries 22, 35
Bowlby, John 2
briefings 39
British Association of Social Workers (BASW)
    3–4, 127
Britton, Ron 25

budgets 69, 94, 95–96, 98, 99, 114; *see also*
    funding; resources

Care Act (2014) 11–12, 96, 110, 126
care homes 75, 87–88
care management 22–23, 56, 95
carers: abuse by 28; participation of 39
case discussions 107, 118, 129
Central Council for Education and Training in
    Social Work (CCETSW) 7, 11
cerebral palsy 17
Certificate of Qualification in Social Work
    (CQSW) 4
change, organisational 66, 86
Chief Social Workers 8, 11, 12, 81, 123, 126
child protection 10–11, 13, 43–44, 73, 95,
    120, 124
Child Protection Task Force 11
children 1–3, 115, 117; Chief Social Worker
    for 11, 12; 'no recourse' cases 72–73;
    parental relationships 23–26; risk assessment
    126
Climbié, Victoria 10, 11, 12, 43, 44–45, 66
College of Social Work 11, 121
commercial agencies 7
commissioner-provider reorganisation 7
community care 5, 53, 114, 116, 118–119
Community Care Act (1990) 11, 95, 96
Community Care (Delayed Discharges) Act
    (2003) 55, 74, 90
confidentiality 12, 26
conflict 62–63
Connelly, Peter ('Baby P') 10, 44
containment 17–18, 19, 24, 43; Hospital Team
    57; organisational 27–28
continuing care 74–75, 76, 128, 137–138
continuous learning 8, 65, 68, 81–84, 117,
    122, 130, 132

147